PSYCHOLOGICAL TESTING
a practical guide for employers

John Toplis is head of Psychological Services at the Post Office, where aptitude tests form part of the selection procedure for the majority of its 180,000 staff. His previous work at the National Institute of Industrial Psychology and as Director of the Occupational Psychology Unit at Barking College of Technology has involved both the development and assessment of tests and their use for counselling, selection and development in a number of commercial and other organisations. He has been active in the British Psychological Society as a former Chairman of the Occupational Psychology Section and member of the Committee of the Division of Occupational Psychology. He is currently Secretary/Treasurer of the International Test Commission, whose members comprise National Psychological Societies and major test publishers worldwide.

Victor Dulewicz is a Fellow of the British Psychological Society and a member of the Division of Occupational Psychology's Committee. He has worked as an occupational psychologist for Rank Xerox and the Civil Service Selection Board, and was for 9 years Manager of Assessment and Occupational Psychology for the STC Group. Recently he became Director of Assessment Services at Henley, The Management College, and also an independent Management Consultant. He advises many organisations on management assessment and development, especially psychological testing and assessment centres, and has written numerous articles on these subjects.

Clive Fletcher is Head of the Psychology Department at Goldsmiths' College, University of London. A Fellow of the British Psychological Society and a former Chairman of its Occupational Psychology Section, he has acted as a consultant to many organisations on assessment and appraisal as well as writing and researching in this field.

PSYCHOLOGICAL TESTING
a practical guide for employers

John Toplis
Vic Dulewicz
Clive Fletcher

Institute of Personnel Management

First published 1987

Reprinted in 1988

Phototypeset by The Design Team, Ascot
and printed in Great Britain
by LR Printing Services Ltd. Crawley, West Sussex

British Library Cataloguing in Publication Data

Toplis, John
   Psychological testing : a practical guide.
   1. Employees, Rating of —— Great Britain
   2. Mental tests —— Great Britain
   I. Title   II. Dulewicz, Vic
   III.   Fletcher, Clive
   658.3'125'019   HF5549.5.R3

ISBN 0-85292-362-7

Contents

Acknowledgements

I am grateful for the help given by Sonia Ostapjuk who was involved in some of the early planning and drafting, and the support given by Richard Osmond and Sandra Davis. Bernard Ungerson CBE, a Past President of the Institute of Personnel Management, made detailed and extremely helpful comments on a draft manuscript, while Dr Kenneth Miller, Director of the Independent Assessment & Research Centre and a Past President of the International Test Commission, reviewed the final manuscript.

John Toplis
London, 1987

The views expressed by the authors are their own and not necessarily shared by the organizations that employ them. The illustrations of good and bad practice that are given are based on their considerable experience as consultants to a wide variety of organizations, and should not be attributed to their employing organizations or other organizations with which they are currently associated.

Foreword

It is not uncommon these days for managers to receive hundreds of applications from a single job advertisement. After even the most stringent pre-selection procedures, these may still only be reduced to a dozen, seemingly equally well-qualified candidates. At this point a manager may for the first time begin to consider the possibility of using psychological testing.

This book has been written for the manager in this position. It has also been written for personnel practitioners who may wish to introduce psychological testing, but whose knowledge or experience of the subject is either rusty or non-existent. After all, although the interview continues to be the favoured method by which people are selected for careers, jobs, promotion and sometimes even redundancy, its shortcomings as a fair and objective basis for such decisions are considerable. Furthermore, these shortcomings are multiplied when an interview panel is involved.

Psychological tests, like most useful tools, need skillful handling to produce maximum benefit. At the same time, managers also need to develop an awareness of the responsibilities involved in the use of tests. Although ignorance of the harm that can be done by unskilled interpretation and feedback of results may be understandable, it must be dispelled.

This is not a textbook, nor is it a marketing document for one test or a set of tests. Our writers have provided us with a readable, practical book on this important subject. They have sought to avoid jargon and mystique, and they have supplied a sound basis for the commercial considerations that must also be taken into account. On behalf of the Institute of Personnel Management's National Committee for Organization and Manpower Planning, who first commissioned the book, I commend it to you.

Christina Vaughan-Griffiths

Introduction

Several years ago I was asked to advise a company on how to improve its selection of supervisors. Having collected background information it became clear that the problem was a very real one. Over the years, the company's manufacturing process had become more complicated, demanding higher levels of diagnostic skill, staff management, record keeping and reporting. In contrast, selection procedures for supervisors had deteriorated; no longer were they carefully selected, trained and monitored when they supervised for the first time; instead, those willing to help the supervisors out had eventually been put in charge themselves. Several had got to the stage where they could not cope.

My recommendations for a new selection system involving a combination of psychological tests, group discussions and individual interviews brought dramatic results. The system discovered people with talent recruited some years previously who had not been considered as production supervisors. As a group they excelled during training, impressing both company training staff and external examiners; as individuals they were pleased to have been given a chance to show what they could do. The company was also pleased that key vacancies were once again filled by staff of suitable calibre.

From experiences of that kind I have no doubt that effective selection can benefit both employers and employees. For employers, there can be increased output from the same number of employees, and other benefits such as shorter training times and lower labour turnover. For employees, it can mean recognition of potential, higher earnings as a result of higher productivity, greater job satisfaction and greater job security.

Good selection should be effective in yielding these benefits, and efficient in terms of the time and other costs involved. To this end, numerous studies have been carried out to determine the effectiveness of selection procedures as a whole and of the component parts of the procedures, such as aptitude tests and interviews. Results have shown that psychometric instruments can make an important and sometimes unique contribution to the procedures.

For this reason the possibility of using psychological tests as part of a selection procedure should always be considered. However, whether or not, and how, to use the instruments in a particular situation will depend on a very large number of factors including the effectiveness and efficiency of past selections, availability of suitable instruments, the number of applicants, the number of vacancies and so on. By identifying and discussing these factors, this book aims to help personnel managers and others make sound decisions about the use of tests, whether they are considering the introduction of tests for the first time or are reviewing existing procedures for testing.

Chapter 1 is aimed at readers with little or no knowledge of testing; it aims to give an overview by means of basic questions and answers about tests. Chapters 2 and 3 describe the characteristics and technical features of psychological tests and give details of different kinds of tests and outline descriptions of them. Chapter 4 explains how instruments can be obtained while chapter 5 describes possible objectives and strategies for using psychological tests. Chapters 6, 7 and 8 describe stages in introducing tests as part of selection − chapter 6 gives details of choosing tests, while chapter 7 covers planning and implementation and chapter 8 describes how decisions can be made and communicated. Chapter 9 discusses the evaluation of psychological tests, while chapter 10 gives information about some current trends and developments and concludes with details about how readers can keep up to date.

John Toplis
London, 1987

1
An overview: some basic questions and answers

Some readers will be unfamiliar with psychological tests, how they can be used and what benefits they can bring. The following questions and answers are designed to give them an overview of the subject and help them decide what other parts of the book to read.

Q Why do people use psychological tests?

A Psychological tests can help to get suitable people into vacant jobs; correct selection means that people can produce more, earn more, get greater satisfaction, stay longer. The size of the benefits can be greater than many imagine; for example, on some jobs the fastest employees can produce three times more than the slowest. Psychological tests can also be a useful method of 'sifting' when there are a large number of applicants for a few posts.

Q Are psychological tests available for every job?

A No. There are too many different jobs for that to be possible. However, some tests cover groups of related jobs such as those involving different types of sales work. Others cover skills which occur in many jobs such as clerical checking or correctly interpreting graphs and tables. If no 'off the shelf' tests are available, tailor-made tests can be designed if the numbers of applicants and vacancies warrant the costs that will be incurred.

Q So why not use tests in every selection procedure?

A For a number of reasons, several of which may apply in a particular situation. Some of the more common objections to testing are as follows:

- costs (not just the cost of the test materials, but of attending training courses in testing and the absence from other work). However, the benefits of testing can be considerably greater;

- effect on candidates; it is sometimes said (i) that candidates will object to being tested, particularly if they have professional or other qualifications or (ii) that candidates will object to taking part in a procedure which becomes long and demanding because of the inclusion of tests. However, such objections are less often raised by good candidates, who are normally keen to show what they can do;

- resistance from existing employees. Some existing employees may take the view that selection from existing staff should be based on seniority alone; there can also be pressures to recruit relations and friends of existing managers and employees. Both kinds of pressure must be resisted if organizations are to be competitive and efficient;

- because tests may discriminate unfairly. However any part of a selection procedure may discriminate unfairly and it cannot be assumed either that tests will discriminate unfairly or that they will be the part of selection most likely to discriminate. Further, because test administration and scoring are standardized and objective (see chapter 2), tests may be more consistent in their fairness than relatively subjective methods such as the interview.

Q What kind of pay off can I expect from tests?

A Pay off needs to take account of both benefits (eg reducing the turnover of staff and/or recruiting new staff whose productivity is higher) and costs (see chapter 9). Different kinds of tests predict different aspects of future performance. For example:

- aptitude tests involve a series of similar items such as checking figures or understanding paragraphs of information; such tests can be a useful guide to what people are able to do and what skills they might develop;

- trainability tests involve giving candidates a short period of intensive training after which their performance is assessed and any errors of technique noted; as the name implies, the tests can be a useful guide to training course performance in particular;

- personality questionnaires focus on aspects of the personality of candidates, for example the way that they tend to relate to other people and how they feel about themselves;

- questionnaires about attitudes and values explore yet other aspects of candidates.

Q I am interested in better selection, but it all sounds rather complicated. What is the best way forward?

A Read this book to get some background information. Then reflect on any current problems that you may have in recruiting and selecting staff. For example, have you a group of staff whose performance has been poor and/or whose turnover high, and could better selection help to remedy this? If you think it might, why not contact an occupational psychologist for a professional opinion? (See appendix 1.)

Q I am suspicious of experts, particularly psychologists! Can't we just buy some tests and get on with it?

A If you ask around long enough you might be able to get hold of what appear to be tests and 'get on with it'. But bear in mind that tests cannot be judged by appearance alone. For example, some years ago a well known computer company purchased a 'test' which some consultants claimed would measure aptitude for computer programming. What they purchased were examples of sample questions which had been copied from a well known text book on psychology! Bear in mind too that a questionnaire recently sold to managers to help them assess personality was put to scientific investigation and found to be of no value. Why not do the job properly, and contact the British Psychological Society for a list of members of the Division of Occupational Psychology? (See appendix 1.) Alternatively, ask the Institute of Personnel Management which has information both about tests and about consultants and their competence.

3

Q But surely the chances of being misled are small?

A There is a great deal of money to be made from selection methods, and none of the consultants or others selling techniques for assessing staff will lack confidence in their products. Among the methods used to impress potential clients are the following:

- charging very large fees (anything costing that much must be the ultimate selection method!);

- charging low fees and relying on a high volume of sales (you don't need psychologists and expensive training courses — here is something that is practical and self-explanatory!);

- the production of testimonials (any selection method will get it right sometimes — so are the tesimonials from people who are expert in the evaluation of selection methods?);

- the production of lists of references to publications and articles (remember that some scientific and professional journals have an editorial advisory panel of experts to help to check the worth of claims made; in contrast, other journals and magazines may not seek such technical advice and may only be interested in articles likely to increase their circulation);

- the production of books which endorse the technique or approach (again, sales may have been the main editorial consideration);

- the idea that the technique can reveal 'the truth' about the candidate, getting behind what the candidate would wish to be known and perhaps even revealing information unknown to the candidate; the origins of 'the truth' may be the time and date of birth of the candidate, appearance, body movements and gestures, handwriting and so on; often the need for training in the techniques is emphasized;

- the need for training is often emphasized for other techniques including those which may originate from or be associated with clinical psychology; again, the appeal of such techniques is the belief that they will help to reveal 'the truth';

- the offer of a free trial of the methods, usually involving the person who will decide whether or not the technique will be used. The consultants are obtaining a degree of commitment by the trial itself; whatever the picture given few are likely to argue with it (see chapter 4);

- the production of spurious scientific evidence; many managers do not understand the key terms 'reliability' and 'validity' which are used in assessment of selection procedures, and this lack of knowledge can be exploited; for example, managers may relax simply because these key words have been used and not check that they have been used properly. The effect may be compounded if statistics are added — fewer still can judge whether the statistics are appropriate;

- by presenting the methods well; it seems to add to the credibility of the procedure if, for example, the assessment involves the use of a small business computer and the results can be presented on a computer printout and/or in the form of a profile.

Since many reputable psychological tests have at least some of the above characteristics it is virtually impossible for the untrained manager to distinguish between selection methods which are valid and those which are not (see chapter 2). Many well-known industrial and other organizations are currently using unproven methods.

2
What are tests?
I   Characteristics and technical features

This chapter gives a brief history of psychological tests and goes on to outline the characteristics and technical features of psychological tests and questionnaires. It comprises the following sections:

- Brief history

- What is a psychological test?

- Properties of psychological tests

- Availability of psychological tests

Brief history

Psychological tests are not, as some people believe, a new and questionable management device imported from the US. It is just over 100 years since Sir Francis Galton published *'Inquiries into Human Faculty and its Development'*, and 80 years since Binet, a Frenchman, constructed the first intelligence test, a forerunner of today's ability tests.

Personality questionnaires have been around almost as long. The first such instrument used as a selection tool was Woodworth's Personal Data Sheet, a rough screening device for identifying seriously neurotic men who would be unfit for the American Army during the first world war. Indeed, the two world wars provided a major impetus to testing, recruiters on both sides of the Atlantic being faced with a massive need for assessments, and very little time. Tests and questionnaires were used to allocate men to posts most appropriate to their abilities and as part of the procedure to select officers.

Following the second world war, there was steady growth in the use of tests in the United States in both the public sector and by private organizations. However, in the early 1960s the growth was checked because of stringent equal opportunities legislation, and fear of court action while the legal situation was clarified. Subsequently there appears to have been a resurgence of interest and application. For example, a survey from the American Society for Personnel Administration, reported in *Personnel Management* in April 1987, shows that a growing number of US companies are using tests. The largest increase has been in the area of personality and psychological testing; in 1986 32 per cent of companies surveyed used such tests, compared with 22 per cent in 1985. Recent research into the costs and benefits of selection has shown that major improvements can result from testing.

In the United Kingdom, the main test users have been the Forces, the Civil Service and some large public corporations, although significant numbers of private organizations have also used tests quite extensively. In both the UK and the US, a considerable increase in test usage by the private sector has been apparent over the last five or six years.

There are now more than 5,000 psychological instruments produced in the English language, but the vast majority of these are available for use by qualified psychologists only.

What is a psychological test?

The British Psychological Society (BPS) has a key role in controlling the publication of professionally-produced test materials. In 1983 a BPS Bulletin contained the following definition of a test:

> The term psychological test refers to a procedure for the evaluation of psychological functions. Psychological tests involve those being tested in solving problems, performing skilled tasks or making judgements. Psychological test procedures are characterized by standard methods of administration and scoring. Results are usually quantified by means of normative or other scaling procedures[1] but they may also be interpreted qualitatively by reference to psychological theory.

1 These terms are explained later in this chapter.

Included in the term psychological test are tests of varieties of: intelligence; ability; aptitude; language development and function; perception; personality; temperament and disposition; and interests, habits, values and preferences.

The BPS definition thus embraces a wide range of tests and questionnaires under the overall heading of psychological tests. This book will concentrate on those instruments which are available to non-psychologists and for which training is available; however other instruments which are of value in occupational assessment but can be used only by accredited psychologists will be mentioned from time to time.

Properties of psychological tests

This section deals with the fundamentals of psychological tests which distinguish them from the plethora of other paper and pencil instruments used in personnel and training departments. For a more detailed treatment of the nature and construction of psychological tests, see Anastasi (1982) or Kline (1986).

At this point it would be useful to differentiate 'psychological tests' between psychometric tests and psychometric questionnaires. Cronbach (1984) has proposed a useful distinction between tests of maximum performance, eg mental ability tests, and tests of habitual performance, eg personality questionnaires. Tests of maximum performance usually measure intelligence or special abilities, and have correct answers so that, broadly speaking, the higher the score the better the performance; as a group, such tests are called 'psychometric tests' during the remainder of this book when specific reference is necessary.

In contrast, tests of habitual performance (questionnaires) tend to be designed to measure personality characteristics, interests, values or behaviour, and therefore an ability is not being stretched to get a high score. With questionnaires a high or a low 'score' signifies the extent to which a person possesses such qualities as co-operation or determination and the appropriateness of the replies will depend on the vacancy to be filled. Some questionnaires measure bi-polar scales, such as Introversion—Extroversion; replies indicate an individual's position on each scale; as a group, such tests will be called 'psychometric questionnaires' during the remainder of this book when specific reference is necessary.

Psychometric tests and questionnaires share the same essential properties. First, they tend with a few exceptions (beyond the scope of this book) to be objective, standardized measures — they require a highly controlled, uniform procedure for administration and scoring. For every candidate, the test items and instructions should be the same; the time allowed should be the same if it is a timed test; the physical test conditions should be the same, ie adequate lighting, a comfortable temperature, no distractions whatsoever, plenty of work space; and so on.

A second feature of proper ability and other psychometric tests is that the test items will be ordered in level of difficulty so that candidates can get settled into the test more easily and weaker ones are not faced with overly complex items early on. They have an opportunity to demonstrate what they are able to do. The difficulty level is determined objectively during the pilot (design) stage of construction by calculating the percentage of those taking the test who got an item correct. In the final versions of the tests, items are re-ordered according to these percentages so that, for example, an item which 95 per cent of the pilot sample got correct would be placed very early on whereas an item which was answered correctly by only 5 per cent of the sample would come very close to the end; thus, when there are time limits, only people with a very high ability at this type of problem are faced with such a difficult item.

Third, psychometric tests and questionnaires are usually objectively scored. The administrator has a key which contains the right answers for the test, or the value to be given to a specific answer on a multiple-choice questionnaire. Thus, with objectively scored instruments, the scorer's judgement does not lead to variations in score, and indeed many instruments these days can also be machine-scored (see chapter 10).

A fourth major determinant of objectivity and standardization is the way in which score is interpreted. The number of items correct on an ability test, or the sum of values for responses on a questionnaire scale, constitute a raw score which has significance only when it is compared to the range of scores obtained from a large representative sample of people for whom the test was designed. The sample might be drawn from the general population or from more specific groups, such as UK graduates or craft apprentices, and is known as the standardization sample. The results constitute norms which, as the name implies, relate all scores to the normal or average performance of the group, and the degrees of deviation above and below the average. It is important that precise information is given about the way that the norms were drawn up — for example, norms for 'supervisors' could be based on those working as supervisors, those appointed as supervisors, those called to a selection procedure for supervisors, or all applicants for supervisory work.

A normative score is read from a norms table and is not open to the subjective interpretation of the tester. The most widely used normative scale is the percentile score which is a rank order scale reflecting the proportion of the reference group who obtained a lower score than the individual being tested. So if a graduate applicant scored at the 65th percentile on a particular test, using UK graduate norms, his score would be better than 65 per cent of UK graduates.

A fifth characteristic of psychometric instruments is that they should have manuals which contain scientific, objective data to demonstrate how good the test is, and to what extent it does what it is supposed to do. Two critical concepts are the test's reliability and validity. Reliability refers to stability and consistency of results obtained and it can be assessed in several different ways. In the 'test-retest' method of assessing reliability a large group of people is tested and then retested, using the same test, about four weeks later. The initial experience of doing the test is likely to improve the group performance on the second occasion; however, if the relative positions of individual scores are found to be very different on the two occasions, the reliability of the test would be suspect.

A good test manual will contain empirical evidence of the test-retest reliability showing the degree of similarity between the results obtained from the first and second administration of the tests to the same sample, and also the degree of internal consistency, using the split half method. This involves comparing the scores obtained on one half of the items (normally the odd-numbered items) to the scores obtained on the other half (the even-numbered items). This figure will reflect the internal consistency of the test, ie whether or not its items all measure the same broad characteristic.

During the design stage of a reputable psychometric instrument great care is taken to ensure that only the items which are measuring the same broad ability are retained for a specific scale. As part of this process, attention needs to be paid to the way that the questions are presented; for example, if some of a trial group were to get all the items of a similar format wrong it would be a sign that these items might be measuring a separate ability, and the possibility would need to be checked.

The sixth characteristic of a psychometric instrument is that its validity has been objectively assessed. Validity is undoubtedly the most important question when choosing a test for occupational assessment and is a measure of how far the test measures what it was designed to measure. In the occupational context, validity is usually demonstrated by relating the score on a test given prior to employment to some sort of external measure of work performance, eg appraisal ratings of job performance, or quasi-objective measures such as performance on a training course, where successful completion of the course is a prerequisite for job success.

If the performance measure is obtained some time after the test has been taken, the validity measure that can be calculated is the predictive validity. This is the extent to which a test can predict future behaviour because it takes account of the wide range of factors that a job incumbent is exposed to, and influenced by. Predictive validity is regarded as the best single measure of the worth of a test.

There are often a number of practical reasons, especially time pressure, why it is not possible to do a predictive validation study, and so a concurrent study (in which the test and performance measures are taken at the same time by existing staff) has to suffice. While concurrent validity gives a fairly good indication of the relevance of a test to work performance, it is not as good a measure as a predictive validity because the test performance of existing staff may be affected by skills and other behaviours acquired during the current employment rather than aptitude or trainability.

When selecting a psychometric test or questionnaire for a specific purpose the most important data in the manual are those relating to validity. Look to see if the instrument shows good validity data on a group of employees similar to the one which you wish to assess; try not to rely on job titles alone as these can be misleading — for example, in the Post Office, executive grade staff are middle managers rather than top managers. Ideally the number involved in the validation study should be at least 100 and the correlation between test scores and the criteria of performance should be at least 0.2 (see chapter 6). If the correlation is lower, it is unlikely that the use of the test will be financially worthwhile (see chapter 9).

One final issue on validity is that of face validity which refers to the extent to which the instrument looks as of it is measuring something relevant to the job. Unfortunately psychometric tests and questionnaires are sometimes judged only on their appearances and as the graphic design of some unproven 'tests' is at least as good as the best of the proven tests, errors of judgement can be made. Face validity is nevertheless of some importance — if an instrument has low face validity or contains items which might, for example, appear bizarre or intrusive to respondents, then its acceptability to candidates will be questionable and this might well affect their motivation and hence undermine the validity of the results. For example, the use of 'inkblots' test on graduates or managers often arouses reactions of mirth, irritation or even hostility and can affect their attitude not only to the specific test but to the entire test procedure.

Information on face validity does not usually appear in psychometric test and questionnaire manuals. In this matter, users have to exercise their own judgement about the potential suitability of an instrument to a particular group of employees. One way round this problem (and another problem when it is not possible to validate an instrument) is to look for an instrument which measures the same characteristic (as denoted by a statistically significant correlation) as another which has already been shown to be valid on a similar group. Most manuals contain the correlations between the test or questionnaire and other similar instruments. If the new instrument is more acceptable, and correlates highly with the unacceptable one, then this can be used in its place with some confidence. Nevertheless, a specific validation study should still be set up wherever possible.

In summary, a 'true' psychometric test or questionnaire can be distinguished in the following ways:

- it is supplied by a reputable publisher only to those who have received training in its use;

- it is supplied with instructions for administration, scoring and interpretation (including norms);

- it is supplied with details of its reliability and validity.

In addition, the 'face validity' of an instrument can be important in determining its acceptability to both the candidates and others who have to endorse the selection process and make use of information arising from it.

Under normal circumstances, managers should only use 'true' tests. When this is not possible or practicable, they should retain an occupational psychologist to identify, trial and evaluate possible new tests (see appendix 1).

Availability of psychological tests

The BPS, with the full support and understanding of the reputable test suppliers[1], exercises rigorous control over who can use what tests, and the standard of training required and given. There are very good reasons why such controls are required. Proper tests are carefully designed and developed and unless they are used by fully qualified or adequately trained staff, their value will be strictly limited and their security jeopardized. Non-psychologists who reach the required standard on courses approved by the BPS are called 'accredited users'.

There are different classes of courses for non-psychologists to enable them to develop their skills and competencies as they progress from one stage of training to the next.[2] Class I courses are designed for those in the personnel and training function who need to administer and score tests for other more qualified, and

1 Each publisher, while maintaining the distinction between different types of tests and the training required to have access to them, describes the classification in its own way. For example, NFER—Nelson now have a system which can be test specific, ie a person can be identified as qualified to use only a single test.

2 With the imminent granting of chartered status to psychologists, it is intended that the only acceptable courses will be those directed by chartered psychologists. At that time, the BPS will not specifically accredit individual courses. It will, however, continue to provide guidelines for acceptable courses.

probably more senior, colleagues who have been trained on Class II courses and who must supervise their work. Courses for these test administrators last two to three days.

Class II courses provide the basic qualification for using ability and aptitude tests (which the BPS describes as 'P' level) for occupational assessment, and last for a minimum of five days, usually with a follow-up day after about six months of experience so that trainees can consolidate their knowledge and experience by discussing actual case studies. After more extensive experience the user is then in a better position to be able to decide if personality questionnaires (which the BPS describe as 'Q' level) would be of value, which is why the BPS specifies a time period, which can be up to 18 months, between completion of a Class II P course and acceptance onto a Q level course. These courses tend to be geared specifically to particular tests and readers are advised to contact specific training institutes for information. A list of those which run Class I and II, P and Q level, is available from the Institute of Personnel Management.

Summary

Psychological tests are well established and a wide choice is available. There is consensus about the technical properties and characteristics to be checked when choosing a particular test, and the British Psychological Society exercises rigorous control over who can use what tests and the standards of training required and given.

3
What are tests?
II   Types of test and outline descriptions

This chapter begins with a classification of available psychometric tests. The types of tests are then discussed and outline descriptions given of some of the better-known tests in each category. It must be stressed that these illustrative descriptions are not an endorsement of the tests and that their technical qualities and relevance to particular circumstances must be carefully assessed.

The second part of the chapter deals with psychometric questionnaires in a similar way.

Those who wish to have background information about the research into mental abilities from which these tests have been derived should see appendix 1.

Psychometric tests are divided into:

(i)   Tests of attainment

(ii)   Tests of general intelligence

(iii)   Tests of special ability or aptitude
         — tests of aptitude for special kinds of work/job
         — test batteries

Psychometric questionnaires can take the form of:

(iv)   Personality questionnaires

(v)   Interest questionnaires

(vi)   Values questionnaires

(vii)   Other approaches to personality assessment

Psychometric tests

From the section above, it will be clear that there are various broad types of tests of mental ability (maximum performance) available: General Intelligence tests; tests of special aptitude/ability; tests of aptitude for specific jobs; and tests of attainment or proficiency.

(i) Tests of attainment

Tests of attainment, which incidentally are not included in the BPS definition of a test (above) but have similar properties and are widely used, are designed to measure the degree of knowledge and/or skill a person has acquired at a particular point in time. School examinations are one type of such a test. They are very much concerned with experience and learning, and the level of proficiency acquired at certain tasks or skills. Tests of intelligence or aptitude, on the other hand, are designed in theory to provide a measure of an individual's capacity to learn (knowledge and skills) or to perform a skilled task in the future, irrespective of present training and experience. In practice, however, because such tests are based upon tasks incorporating verbal, numerical or symbolic information they rarely, if ever, provide measures which are completely uninfluenced by previous experience and education. It is perhaps helpful to envisage a continuum, with pure attainment tests on one side, say on the left, and pure psychological tests of aptitude on the other, on the right. Thus, a test of mathematical attainment involving knowledge of basic mathematical principles would lie to the left of centre and an O-level maths exam might lie a little further to the left, but neither would be at the end, because the person's numerical reasoning ability would also affect performance on these attainment tests. Similarly, a numerical reasoning test would lie to the right of the continuum, but not quite at the extreme because knowledge and experience of working with figures at school would probably have some effect on performance.

Psychometric tests are therefore designed to assess capacity rather than existing knowledge and skill. To give an understanding of the different types of tests of intelligence, special aptitudes/abilities and tests of aptitudes for specific jobs, examples will be described in sections below. Examples will also be given of the more widely used tests which have proved to be valuable for assessment and counselling purposes. Some tests are designed for use with the general population, to discriminate across the entire ability range, whilst others are designed to discriminate most effectively within specific sections of the range, for example among graduate or management populations; in tests designed for the latter groups the types of mental operations called for are of a much higher order of complexity, such as reasoning and evaluation (Guilford).

When considering tests it is important to look at the tests and the test manuals and not make decisions only on the basis of the test title. In particular, most tests have instructions which demand a knowledge of language, and it is, for example, difficult to design numerical items free of verbal skills.

Tests can either be used alone or in combination with other tests according to the quality or qualites to be measured. Combinations of tests are called test batteries. Some test batteries comprise tests which have been designed for use together and which may have similar instructions, answer sheets, etc. Often a single manual gives details about all the tests in the battery and gives information about combinations of the tests to be used for common vacancies such as those for apprentices or graduate entrants. Following a review of the different broad types of test, test batteries are considered further.

(ii) Tests of general intelligence

There is a multitude of different definitions of intelligence but the simplest and most appropriate for practical purposes is 'the capacity for abstract thinking and reasoning with a range of different contents and media'. The specific scientific identification and measurement of intelligence is nowadays carried out using a statistical technique called factor analysis to determine the general intelligence component across a number of different tests. Further information about mental abilities is given in appendix 1.

It usually takes between 30 and 60 minutes to obtain a reliable measure of general intelligence. Most intelligence (and aptitude) tests are administered to groups, require written responses and are timed. Items are usually presented in verbal, numerical and symbolic/diagrammatic form, thus sampling a range of different formats. The written response normally involves marking one of a number of possible correct answers but a few tests require candidates to write the correct answer (open-ended).

Examples of the more popular types of item format in tests of general intelligence are given below:

Verbal:
(a) Analogies
     Child is to parent as kitten is to....
     (a) Bitch (b) Mouse (c) Cat (d) Terrier (choose one)

(b) Synonyms
     Which of the following means the same as 'tired'
     (a) Fatigued (b) Hot (c) Energetic (d) Stiff (choose one)

Non-verbal:

(a) Number Series
     Fill in the missing number in the series below:
     2 4 7 11 .. 22

(b) Diagrammatic/Symbolic Reasoning
     Which of the following should be added to complete the series of diagrams below; 1, 2 or 3?

Some psychometric tests contain all these types of items, and others as well, whilst some so called 'culture fair' tests contain only symbolic/diagrammatic items in an attempt to overcome the problems associated with candidates from different, non-western cultures and/or those whose first language is not English. This is a major issue in testing and is discussed in chapter 9.

There is a wide variety of tests of general intelligence available, and the choice of which one to use depends largely on the educational level of applicants, their previous experience and the jobs for which they are being considered.

Examples of such tests, designed to discriminate across the general population are:

- AH2/AH3: Verbal, Numerical and Perceptual Items (Source:2[1])

- AH4: slightly higher level than AH2/AH3
  Verbal, Numerical and Diagrammatic Items (Source: 2)

- NIIP Groups tests 70 and 70B: Two almost parallel forms, non-verbal items — coding, matrices and series (Source: 2)

- Ravens Standard Progressive Matrices: A non-verbal test, with diagrammatic items, in matrix form (Sources: 2, 6)

These tests are all British, with extensive British norms available. Three American tests which are widely used and well validated but for which only American norms appear in the manuals are:

- Otis-Lennon Mental Ability Test — Advanced Level: Verbal, Numerical and Diagrammatic items (Sources: 5, 6)

- Thurstone Test of Mental Awareness: Verbal and Numerical items (Source: 4)

- Cattell Culture Fair Intelligence Test (Scale 2): Non-verbal items in four sub tests, covering series, classification, incomplete designs and evaluations (Source: 2)

The tests above are designed for individuals with average ability and are suitable for general personnel selection. However, if one needs to assess the general intelligence of clearly above-average individuals like graduates, managers and research staff the following tests are more suitable:

- AH5/AH6: Verbal, numerical and diagrammatic items. AH6 has two equivalent forms, one for scientists, engineers and mathematicians, the other for those with an arts background (Source: 2)

- Compound Series Test: A non-verbal test with diagrammatic items (Source: 1)

- Ravens Advanced Progressive Matrices: A non-verbal test with diagrammatic items, in matrix form. Unlike the others, it

1   Details of the test publishers referenced in the text are in appendix 3.

can be used as a test of intellectual power alone, independent of speed (Sources: 2, 6)

(iii) Tests of special aptitude or ability

From the early years of intelligence testing some psychologists considered that important information about an individual's ability was being obscured by concentrating on only one score, of general intelligence, and started looking at candidates' performance on specific types of items such as verbal or numerical questions (see appendix 2). This trend was accelerated by Thurstone's identification of the seven primary mental abilities. For many years, test developers have concentrated their efforts on producing tests which measure and produce a single score for a specific mental ability, which is statistically reasonably independent of other special abilities. Such scores are not completely independent of each other because the influence of general intelligence also contributes to varying degrees, depending on the actual test, to a special ability score.

The terms 'special ability' or 'special aptitude' are often used imprecisely and interchangeably. A 'special aptitude' is a capacity for performing a specific group of tasks which have been shown to be highly related to each other statistically. The term 'special ability' is often used in the same sense, based upon its use in the theories of mental ability of both Thurstone and Vernon, where ability for special tasks is contrasted with general intellectual ability across all mental tasks. There are also aptitude tests for specific types of work, such as computer programming, which often combine different subtests of special abilities to provide an overall score which reflects the capacity to do a specific type of work. Some examples of aptitude tests for specific types of jobs are described below and are classified both by content, viz verbal, numerical, spatial, diagrammatic/symbolic — and by level, viz for lower level and higher level ability.

Examples of tests for special aptitude/ability

(a)   Verbal ability. There are a number of tests which measure lower levels of verbal (word) meaning and comprehension, some of which also necessitate an element of reasoning with words. All tests in this section have British norms:

- Personnel Tests for Industry: Verbal (Source: 5)
- VPI Verbal Usage (Source: 3)
- VTI Verbal Comprehension (Source: 2)

Verbal tests involving significantly more complex mental operations of reasoning and critical evaluation are available for assessing candidates of high ability such as graduates and managers:

- Watson-Glaser Critical Thinking Appraisal Forms Ym, Zm, A and B (Source: 5)
- GMA Verbal Test (Source: 2)
- VA1 Verbal Concepts (Source: 3)
- VA3 Verbal Test (Source: 2)

(b) Numerical Ability. Lower level numerical tests often involve an understanding of and skill at arithmetical calculations and so candidates' existing attainments are being assessed as well as their aptitude:

- General Clerical Test — Numerical (Source: 5)
- NP2 and NT2 Numerical Computation (3)
- NP6 Numerical Reasoning (3)
- Personnel Tests for Industry — Numerical (5).

As with the verbal tests, there are also numerical tests for candidates of high ability such as graduates, and potential or actual supervisors and managers; these assess higher order numerical reasoning and critical evaluation of quantitative information:

- GMA Numerical Test (Source: 2)
- NA2 Number Series (3)
- NC2 Interpreting Data (3)
- NA4 Numerical Critical Reasoning (3).

(c) Spatial Ability. Candidates are required to work mentally to

identify, visualise, compare and/or manipulate two or three dimensional shapes. Such ability has a lower general intelligence component than many of the other abilities and is therefore a more distinct, purer ability.

Tests for lower level applicants include:

- ET3 Visual Estimation (Source: 3)

- NIIP Group Test 82 (2)

- Revised Minnesota Paper Form Board Test (5)

- ST9 Spatial Recognition (3).

Two tests for higher ability candidates, which include three dimensional shapes are:

- ST7 Spatial Reasoning (Source: 3)

- Shapes Analysis Test (6).

(d) Diagrammatic Ability. These tests do not include verbal or numerical items but include abstract symbols and diagrams, covering a range of operations from fairly superficial perceptual to complex abstract, logical processes. Some designers argue that they are not dependent on attainment and so are purer measures of reasoning, but it is debatable whether they are 'culture free' or 'culture fair'. We will return to this complex argument later. Examples of lower level diagrammatic tests are:

- NIIP Group Tests 70 and 70B (Source: 2)

The following tests are more appropriate for higher ability candidates, such as technicians, scientists and engineers:

- Culture Fair Intelligence Test, Scale 3 (Source: 2)

- DT8 Diagrammatic Reasoning (3)

- DA5 Diagramming (3)

- GMA Abstract (2).

(e) Mechanical Ability. This ability incorporates an element of

intelligence and reasoning and is entirely separate from manual dexterity (see below). Inevitably, there is a knowledge component (elementary physics) and so the tests are not pure ability tests, but manuals do include evidence that they provide a measure of the capacity to learn and to succeed at certain jobs requiring mechanical ability and hence are tests of aptitude. Examples of mechanical aptitude tests are:

- ACER Mechanical Reasoning (Source: 2)
- Mechanical Comprehension Tests (2)
- MT4 Mechanical Comprehension (3)
- NIIP Vincent Mechanical Diagrams Test (2).

(f)   Manual Dexterity. Eye-hand co-ordination is obviously relevant to most manual tasks and research has shown that these abilities are not closely related to intelligence or to the abilities listed above. Indeed, there is a range of such fairly specific abilities requiring perception and manipulation involving fingers and hands. Some tasks require speed and little precision whilst with others extreme precision is of paramount importance. Because such abilities are specific, it is necessary to carry out a careful analysis of the job before deciding on what test is most appropriate. Indeed many successful tests are more akin to job samples or job simulations. However, some dexterity tests are available including the following:

- Bennett Hand Tool Dexterity Test, for assessing proficiency with conventional tools like spanners and screwdrivers; (Source: 2)
- Crawford Small Parts Dexterity Test (5)
- Fine Dexterity Test (6)

  The Crawford and Fine Tests measure performance on precision tasks using small tools
- Purdue Pegboard (4). This test measures two kinds of finger dexterity from gross movement to finger-tip dexterity.

Two pencil and paper tests designed to measure dexterity are:

- Flanagan Industrial Test (FIT) Co-ordination and Precision (Source: 4)

- EITS Speed Test (Speed and Precision) (1).

Examples of tests of aptitude for specific types of work/jobs

(a) Clerical Speed and Accuracy. For many lower level office jobs, especially clerical jobs, an aptitude for identifying, comparing and checking similarities or differences of numerical, verbal or symbolic information is a requirement. This aptitude can also be one component requirement of a few higher level jobs as well, even though it is largely independent of general intelligence. There are a number of clerical tests available:

- ACER Speed and Accuracy Test (Source: 2)

- CP3 Checking (3)

- CP7 Basic Checking (3)

- CP8 Audio Checking (Oral Information) (3)

- EITS Clerical 1 (1).

There have of course been major changes in the nature of office work in recent years. The increased use of electronic equipment in the office of today has been shown to require higher level checking and coding aptitudes. The following tests are relevant:

- CC2 Computer Checking (Source: 3)

- C13 Coded Instructions (3)

- NEI Numerical Estimation. (3)

(b) Word processor aptitude. The use of word processors requires an aptitude distinct from typing skills. The following battery measures aptitude for basic WP tasks and aptitude for advanced tasks:

- EOSYS Word Processing Aptitude Battery (Source: 3)

Other test for word processing are:

24

- EITS Information Systems Skills (Source: 1)
- SRA Word Processor Battery (1).

(c)   Computer Aptitude. Computer programming requires aptitudes to cope with the special forms of logical reasoning required.
One tailor-made battery comprising five sub-tests which has been
in use for over 20 years and is well validated across many different
programming jobs is the:

- Computer Programmer Aptitude Battery (Sources: 2, 4).

Many users have used different combinations of general intelligence and special ability tests to identify programming aptitude —
the capacity to learn and subsequently apply programming skills.
It should be stressed that none of these tests should be used to
identify higher-order programming skills in experienced programmers. A programming aptitude battery from various other batteries has been developed and validated, with different combinations
of tests for different types of programming. This is the:

- PAS Programming Aptitude Series (Source: 3).

The capacity for operating computer hardware is distinct from
programming and a battery has been developed and validated to
assess this specific aptitude, consisting of three sub-tests:

- COAB Computer Operator Aptitude Battery (Source: 4).

(d)   Language Aptitude. The capacity to learn foreign languages
is an aptitude that has been identified by research studies. The
following test will probably be of interest to organizations which
need to train staff to use a number of different foreign languages:

- Modern Language Aptitude Battery (Source: 2).

Test Batteries
At the beginning of this chapter, there was mention of batteries of
tests comprising tests designed to be used together and which

cover a wide range of special abilities and aptitudes for specific purposes.

Most of these have been referred to in the sections above. For selecting managers and graduates, there are the Advanced Test Battery from SHL and the Graduate and Management Battery from NPER-Nelson; the Technical Test Battery for apprentices and engineering technicians from SHL; and the Personnel Test Battery for office staff from SHL. There are also Differential Ability batteries which are used widely for selection and which are particularly valuable for counselling purposes.

Differential batteries provide not only a score for each specific ability but also look at the relative scores of an individual across a profile to determine a person's relative strengths and weaknesses. Such batteries can be especially valuable for vocational guidance and counselling, and for placement purposes — allocating a person to a particular job from a choice of many to maximize his/her strengths, and the job/person match. Individual tests or combinations of tests from the batteries are often used for selection purposes. Of the differential batteries which cover a wide range of activities, the most widely used are:

- Differential Aptitude Tests (Source: 5)

- Morrisby Differential Test Battery (1).

Personality assessment and psychometric questionnaires

The term 'personality' is all-embracing in terms of the individual's behaviour and the way it is organized and co-ordinated when he or she interacts with the environment. The sorts of personality characteristics which are normally asessed include emotional adjustment, social relations, motivation, interests, values and attitudes. However, some psychologists believe that cognitive processes (eg intelligence) should also be taken into account when looking at the total personality and so have included cognitive scales within their questionnaires.

While psychologists agree that specific aspects of an individual's personality, such as interests, motivations, values and attitudes are also relevant to occupational assessment and guidance, there are different views about how these aspects relate with one another. Some psychologists see them as overlapping to various degrees with an individual's personality. Others propose a hierarchical model, with personality traits at the bottom, influencing and determining values which in turn influence interests and motivations. These ultimately produce attitudes and a predisposition to behave in certain ways.

Within such a complex and wide-ranging field of study, there are obviously different theories of personality. Below there follow descriptions of the different methods of assessment, rather than descriptions of the theories themselves; for a brief account of the latter, see Shackleton and Fletcher (1984).

Self-report personality questionnaires

These are of particular relevance to this book because the large majority of instruments used for occupational assessment of personality, motivations, interests, attitudes and values are self-report questionnaires. Furthermore, as already noted, some are available for use in the UK by non-psychologists provided that they are accredited users (see chapter 2).

The foundations underlying personality questionnaires are the 'trait' or 'type' theories which are closely related. The trait approach involves the identification of a number of fairly independent and enduring characteristics of behaviour which all people display but to differing degrees. An example of such a trait is sociability, with a scale from extremely sociable to not sociable at all. Expressed in its simplest form, what trait theorists like Cattell and Guilford have done is to identify examples of common behaviour, devise scales to measure these and then obtain ratings on these behaviours by people who know each other well. These observations have then been analysed statistically, using Factor Analysis, to generate broad traits to be found together, but are fairly independent of other traits. Groups of traits which are associated, but more loosely, go to make up personality 'types'.

Some of the words used to describe traits are also common in everyday language — examples are introvert and extravert, stable and anxious. When choosing and using questionnaires, it is important to study the designer's definitions of the traits. Not only may there be important differences between the designer's definitions and those assumed by potential users, but there can also be differences in the way that the same terms have been defined by different designers. Certainly, traits with similar titles can reflect quite different behaviour. Accordingly the author's definition of a particular trait must always be referred to in order to obtain a clear impression of what behaviour the trait actually represents.

Questionnaires have been developed to measure these specific aspects of personality, and the choice of which instrument to use depends largely on the nature of the information users decide to be most relevant to their purposes and objectives. Below are examples of the various instruments which are available to non-psychologists who have completed Q-level training (see chapter 2). Because of the wide range of questionnaires available and constraints on space in this book, only the most widely used and validated questionnaires have been included.

(iv) Personality questionnaires

(a) Cattell's 16 PF

The 16 Personality Factor questionnaire was developed over 36 years ago in the US initially for research and clinical purposes. However, for many years it has been used for general personality assessment and an enormous amount of research into its technical properties and its applications has been carried out. Detailed results are published in the 16 PF Handbook. There are four forms for general use, each with British norms: Forms A and B, which are full versions, and C and D which are shorter versions, with simpler language for those with low educational attainment. All forms measure the same 16 primary factors and four second-order factors: introversion-extroversion; emotional stability; tough-poise; and independence. The test handbook also contains numerous empirically derived indices of job-related criteria such as accident proneness, leadership, creativity and many others.

The questionnaire is used for both occupational assessment and counselling. All versions are untimed and take between 25 and 60 minutes to complete. (Source: Cattell's 16 PF Forms A, B, C and D and High School; Source: 2).

(b) Gordon Personal Profile and Inventory

This is a well established instrument with much technical data contained within its manual. It has two parts. The Profile measures ascendancy, responsibility, emotional stability and sociability and the Inventory measures cautiousness, original thinking, personal relations and vigour. It is untimed, and each part usually takes

15-20 minutes to complete. It is useful for both counselling and assessment in an occupational setting. The norms in the manual are American (Sources: 2, 6).

(c)   Saville and Holdsworth's (SHL) Occupational Personality Questionnaire (OPQ)

The OPQ was published in 1984 after four years of systematic development in the UK. It is designed specifically to assess personality characteristics in the world of work for assessment and counselling purposes. There are 10 different versions, with various response formats used in each version. Therefore, some are more suitable for selection purposes, others for counselling. The main domains of personality measured by the OPQ are: relationships with people; thinking style; and feelings and emotions. The longest form, Concept Model, assesses 30 primary factors and takes about 60 minutes to complete, whilst the shortest, Pentagon, measures five dimensions and takes about 10 minutes. The manual contains British norms for all versions based on the standardization sample of managerial and professional employees. British graduate norms are also available for some versions. Extensive reliability data on all versions are also presented. Supplements to the manual, covering additional norms and research data are produced on a regular basis (Source: 3).

(d)   Myers-Briggs Type Indicator

This American personality questionnaire has been developed over the last 40 years and is based on Jung's theory of types. It contains four scales: introversion-extroversion; sensing-intuition; thinking-feeling; and judging-perceptive. Scores can be reported as continuous variables or as a specific type code. There are two versions, Form F and a shorter Form G which are both untimed and usually take around 40 and 30 minutes respectively to complete. The Indicator is used primarily in personal counselling, although there is also limited evidence of its value as a selection aid. The manual contains American norms for interpretations (Sources: 2, 6).

(v)   Interest questionnaires

These have usually been designed for vocational and career guidance purposes although most instruments have been used for selection purposes, with some positive results. They are designed for use with teenagers and adults.

(a) Strong-Campbell Interest Inventory

This American questionnaire which has been developed over the last 50 years surveys attitudes to a large number of different jobs. Responses are compared with successful men and women in a wide range of occupations and scores are produced for six general themes, 23 basic interest scores (eg public speaking) and 207 occupational scores. The questionnaire takes 15 to 30 minutes to complete. A manual and user's guide are available, containing American data (Source: 2).

(b) Rothwell-Miller Interest Blank

This questionnaire was first published in Australia in 1958; a British edition was published in 1968 with UK data. There are two versions of the questionnaire, one for male and one for female subjects, who rank occupations which represent 12 general areas of interest. The results reflect respondents' preferences for particular types of occupations. It is primarily a counselling instrument but is also used for selection (especially apprentice) and placement purposes. It takes about 20 minutes to complete. Revised and unisex versions are now being trialled (Source: 2).

(c) Vocational Preference Inventory

This American Inventory, designed by Holland, is self-administered and takes between 30 and 45 minutes to complete. Respondents indicate which occupations they think they would like or dislike and 11 scales are measured: realistic, intellectual, social, conventional, enterprising, artistic, self-control, masculinity, status, infrequency, and acquiescence. It is essentially a counselling instrument and the manual contains male and female American norms (Source: 2).

(d) SHL General Occupational Interest Inventory

This British questionnaire is designed for those with low or no formal educational qualifications and takes about 35 minutes to complete. Individuals state whether they like a number of activities related to specific jobs. Eighteen scores are provided, including people, office, control, leisure and practical. The manual provides British standardization data. The Inventory is used primarily for counselling but also for selection and placement

(Source: 3).

(e)   SHL Advanced Occupational Interest Inventory
This British questionnaire, designed for adolescents with O Levels and above, is also used for employees in graduate and management positions. There is no time limit but it normally takes about 35 minutes to complete. Respondents provide their preferences for a number of relevant job activities and scores are produced on 19 categories of interests. The three main domains are people, data and practical interests. British norms are provided in the manual and the inventory is used primarily for counselling, but also for selection and placement (Source: 3).

(f)   SHL Management Interest Inventory
This British Inventory is designed for people currently in, or likely to rise to, management grades. There is no time limit but it normally takes about 30 minutes to complete. Subjects provide information of their experience of various skills and functions and their liking of specific relevant activities. Scores are produced on 12 management functions (eg sales, finance, data processing) and on 12 management skills (eg problem-solving, decision making, organizing and communicating). The inventory is used for counselling, selection and placement purposes and the manual contains British normative data (Source: 3).

(vi)   Values questionnaires

(a)   Gordon Surveys of Values (Personal and Interpersonal)
Each survey covers six values — Interpersonal: support, conformity, recognition, independence, benevolence and leadership. Personal: practical-mindedness, achievement, variety, decisiveness, orderliness and goal-orientation. They are untimed but usually take about 10 minutes each. The Surveys in the UK are used more for employment purposes than for counselling. The manual is American but a UK supplement is in preparation (Source: 4).

(b)   Study of Values
This American questionnaire, devised by Allport, Vernon and Lindsey, has been in use for over 40 years and an Anglicized version has been produced by Richardson. It is designed to measure the relative prominence of six basic interests and values

within personality: theoretical, economic, aesthetic, social, political and religious. It is untimed but normally takes about 20 minutes to complete. The manual, which is available only on microfiche, contains extensive American research normative data. The questionnaire is designed essentially for counselling purposes (Source: 2).

(vii)   Specific work behaviour questionnaires.
Some questionnaires are available which cover very specific work behaviour relating to interpersonal style and other aspects within the broad personality domain. The three specific examples described below are quite widely used in the UK and have sound validity evidences within their manuals.

(a)   Leadership Opinion Questionnaire
The LOQ was devised by Fleishman and is based upon the extensive research studies into leadership carried out in the 1940s and 1950s. It measures the two main independent dimensions of effective leadership: Consideration — rapport and communication with subordinates — and Structure — initiation of ideas and plans, directing groups towards goals. It can be self-administered and takes about 10-15 minutes to complete. It is designed for selection of supervisors and managers and also for counselling and developing trainees for such jobs. The manual contains extensive American norms and research data (Source: 4).

(b)   Poppleton-Allen Sales Aptitude Test (PASAT)
Although this is described as an aptitude test, it is a self-report questionnaire of 'habitual responses' rather than a test of 'maximum response' and so is included in this section. It is designed to measure 15 different sales behaviours and is based upon quite extensive job analysis and factor analytic research on sales staff in the late 1970s. The job behaviour factors cover the areas of social skills, organization and planning, emotional expression and motivation. It is untimed but usually takes 20-30 minutes to complete. It is designed specifically for selection of applicants for sales jobs. The manual contains British norms for different types of selling and other technical data (Source: 6).

(c)   Sales Attitude Checklist
This American questionnaire contains items which reflect attitudes

towards selling and habitual behaviour in the selling situation. It thus measures various attitudes and behaviours relevant to selling. It is untimed, usually takes 10-15 minutes to complete, and a single score is calculated. It is used for the selection of applicants for selling jobs. The manual contains American norms and research data (Source: 4).

(viii) Other Approaches to the Assessment of Personality

(a) Simulation/Situational Tests

One method for assessing personality which is quite widely used is the use of trained assessors to evaluate clearly defined personality characteristics which are described in behavioural terms so that each assessor is looking for exactly the same qualities (eg assertiveness, flexibility, stress tolerance). Assessors watch candidates attempt situational exercises which simulate work at the level at which candidates will be expected to perform in the organization. This approach often forms part of an Assessment Centre, at which candidates are also assessed by other means including interviews and psychological tests. Assessment Centres have been shown to produce the highest predictive validity of any assessment method but, apart from the use of tests, are beyond the scope of this book. However, there is extensive literature on the subject: see Stewart and Stewart (1981) and Thornton and Byham (1982).

(b) Projective techniques

Each candidate is presented with a relatively unstructured task of stimuli which provide wide latitude in terms of response. The assumption underlying such methods is that the candidate will 'project' his or her attitudes, values, motivations and so on into responses to the ambiguous material. These methods have sometimes been effective if used alongside the interview by psychologists with special training. They have the specific advantage that they are disguised in their purpose and so it is very difficult for the subject to present a favourable image or desired impression. Techniques such as sentence completion, the Rorschach 'inkblots' and the Thematic Apperception Test (TAT) have been used in personnel assessment with some evidence of success but they do pose questions about reliability and validity, and there are often major problems about face validity, ie acceptability by candidates, especially questions of relevance. Projective tests are not available to non-psychologists and anyone who wishes to try them out is advised to approach only psychologists with extensive experience of their use in the occupational assessment field.

(c) Objective Tests of Personality

Some psychologists, notably Cattell, have devised experimental laboratory situations to test the hypothesis that psycho-physiological measures, eg heart rate, respiration rate, brain wave patterns, are correlates of personality characteristics. These tests involve either giving subjects a specific task to perform or subjecting them to some kind of specific stimulus, such as the sound of a gun shot, and measuring changes in psycho-physiological patterns. Whilst there is limited evidence that, for example, introverts and extroverts behave differently in some of these test situations, the evidence is not strong, and there are major problems in terms of acceptability to subjects! Such methods have not been used in occupational assessment in the UK, although the polygraph (lie-detector), which is a variant of such psycho-physiological assessment methods, has been introduced recently by a few organizations. Its use has however been strongly criticized by the British Psychological Society. Again such methods are beyond the scope of this book.

(d) Fringe Methods of Personality Assessment

The resurgence of interest in scientific personality assessment has also brought in its wake interest in non-scientific methods such as handwriting analysis (graphology), astrology, palmistry, phrenology and so on. A recent study by Robertson and Makin (1986) showed that 2.6 per cent of the top 1,000 UK companies always used graphology when assessing managers. Yet a major review of the effectiveness of the method by Klimoski and Rafaeli (1983) concluded that, in studies which have been scientifically rigorous, the results have not supported the usefulness of inferences based on handwriting. They concluded, 'given the evidence that we do have a great reliance on inferences based on script must be considered unwarranted'.

Summary

The Purpose of this chapter has been to describe briefly mental abilities and personality, to outline how they can be assessed and to give brief details of some of the better known tests which are available.

It must again be stressed that the illustrative descriptions are not an endorsement of the tests, and that technical qualities and relevance to particular circumstances must be carefully assessed.

4
Obtaining tests

Properly designed psychological tests are supplied only to people trained in their use (see chapter 2). Accordingly, personnel managers and others contemplating the use of tests need to decide how their organizations can get access to the test or tests that may benefit their selections. In practice, there are three main ways of doing this. The first is to have personnel managers or other staff attend one or more training courses in the use of tests. The second is to retain a consultant to advise as appropriate. The third is to employ one or more occupational specialist psychologists. In this chapter, each option is discussed in turn.

Training courses

The British Psychological Society has approved a number of training courses in the use of psychological tests and lists of such courses are available both from the British Psychological Society and from the Institute of Personnel Management. Each of these courses is geared towards specific tests. Therefore an assessment of the likely worth of specific tests will have to be made before actually attending the training courses. Information about the possible benefits of using the test can be obtained from either the training course organizers and/or from the suppliers of the tests featured in the training courses. Note that courses run by test publishers are confined to their own tests, while other trainers normally draw on tests from a number of publishers. In all, about 50 courses have been approved by the British Psychological Society.

It is important that those sent for training in testing to become 'accredited users' have qualities that will enable them to administer, score and interpret the tests successfully, to obtain suitable facilities and equipment for successful testing, and to defend the appropriate introduction and use of tests. A good level of intelligence is also required to understand the principles involved and explain them to others. Thus those sent for training must be able to read the test instructions aloud in a clear voice, be able to mark tests quickly and accurately, be able to collate and total scores, be able to compare scores with others using norm tables, and be able to explain the results to others both orally and in writing. Finally, competence in the basic use of small business computers or computer terminals is of increasing value (see chapter 10). The demands made by Class II training courses are obviously greater than those required by Class I (see chapter 2).

The cost of becoming an 'accredited user' can be considerable. There will certainly be tuition fees and there may well be travelling and residential fees. In addition, there is the cost of absence from work and the cost of obtaining supplies of testing materials.

Once a member of staff is trained, the cost of that person administering a testing programme may be low compared with the other options of regularly involving consultants or employing specialist internal staff, although some test suppliers require registration or licence fees and there is the cost of the test materials too (illustrative costs are given in chapter 9). However, these short training courses cannot give people the considerable expertise required to develop or evaluate sophisticated testing systems, and an occupational psychologist will be required to do this (see below).

Once an organization has accredited users it is sensible that less senior and expensive staff are trained to do the actual administration by attending a Class I course (see chapter 2).

Retaining an independent consultant

Without experience of the use of tests, personnel staff are not in a strong position to decide between testing courses. Accordingly, it may be found useful to obtain advice from a consultant occupational psychologist and those considering this strategy are recommended to approach the British Psychological Society (address at appendix 4) for the directory of members of the Division of Occupational Psychology. By approaching someone outside the organization who is professionally qualified and independent of both the training courses and the supply of tests an impartial view should be obtained. In addition, the psychologist will be able to advise on benefits and costs of developing new tests to meet specific client needs; this can be an attractive strategy if large numbers are to be tested and/or the qualities to be tested are beyond the normal range of tests.

Advice on testing is sometimes offered by consultants and others who are not psychologists. But it is only the British Psychological Society which has drawn up standards about the use of tests, and only the Division of Occupational Psychology which has a Code of Conduct geared to industrial and commercial practice (see appendix 1).

Employing specialist staff

The third alternative is for an organization to consider the appointment of its own occupational psychologist. This again should ensure an impartial assessment of the potential benefits of testing and other assessment methods. However, the commitment to employ an occupational psychologist on anything other than a short term contract will be making assumptions about the value of using tests and about the level of recruitment in the months and years ahead. While the psychologist might be able to contribute to many other aspects of the organization besides selction, the short term and long term role of the psychologist would need to be fully considered before this option were chosen. This strategy is most appropriate when there is scope for large scale testing and assessment and when considerable savings can be made by developing in-house tests and training courses tailor-made to the organization's needs. Major UK organizations employing their own occupational psychologists include the Civil Service, British Telecom, The Post Office and British Airways.

All in all, there may be advantages in seeking advice from an independent occupational psychologist initially and then evaluating the other options in the light of the benefits which testing and the other skills of occupational psychologists are likely to bring (see appendix 1).

Tests from other sources

Because of the cost of obtaining reputable psychological tests, some managers may be tempted to try some of the material available from non-psychologists which are claimed to measure ability, personality etc. Although such materials are often well presented, there is seldom any technical information of the kind described in chapter 2 to back up claims about the value of the techniques. For example, in June 1986 the *Guidance and Assessment Review* (published by the BPS) carred a report of the systematic analysis of two inventories of this kind and concluded that there was little evidence to suggest that either could justify the apparently detailed analysis of personality which the authors claimed of their system of profile analysis.

If these or other instruments are used there is not only the danger that they may select the wrong people, but that their use could not be justified at an industrial tribunal and that the reputation of the employing organization could be severely damaged; mention has already been made of the fact that some tests which fail to meet psychometric standards have appealing graphic design, and those contemplating the use of tests must be careful not to base their judgements on appearances alone.

There are two other reasons why some unproven tests may be widely used. The first is that some managers lack the kind of information available in this book and do not appreciate the kind of information that should be available about a test.

The second reason is the widespread use of a 'ploy' to sell supposed measures of personality; the ploy involves asking managers to complete a questionnaire and subsequently discussing their results with them. The results can seem quite impressive, a powerful and personal demonstration of validity. Unfortunately, it is no such thing.

This was nicely demonstrated in a well-known study by Stagner (1958) who gave a personality inventory to a group of 68 personnel managers at a conference, then took their papers away for scoring. Later, the participants were given a report describing their personality as shown by their results. Fifty per cent rated their report as 'amazingly accurate', 40 per cent as 'rather good', and the remaining ten per cent judged it as 'about half and half'; none rated their reports as 'more wrong than right' or as 'almost entirely wrong'. It was then revealed to the managers involved that they had all in fact been given exactly the same personality description, which was nothing to do with the personality inventory. How could the participants have been so convinced yet so deceived? Nor are they alone. This study has been repeated many times and the same results found, even when the participants have been given reports containing unflattering descriptions of themselves.

This phenomenon is called 'the Barnum effect' after the showman of the same name. It is in effect a trick. The personality descriptions are loaded with vague generalities which are actually applicable to most people; statements like, 'I am sometimes not as confident as I appear'. Not suprisingly, when faced with a whole series of such truisms presented by a consultant or other 'expert' as being the product of a carefully constructed test, people tend to be impressed. After all, what is being given them is for the most part correct as far as it goes; the trouble is, it does not differentiate one person from another and cannot be of any use in decision making.

Something similar happens when you visit a fortune teller ('I see a tall, dark stranger') or when graphologists 'prove' that handwriting analysis is the key to personality assessment by giving a description based on somebody's signature. Although it often goes against the grain to admit it, judging the worth of a personality measure on the basis of one's perceptions of its accuracy in describing oneself is woefully inadequate.

Tests developed outside the UK

Test materials developed in America and other overseas countries sometimes have good technical information but can require substantial adaptation before they can be used with confidence in the UK. Services of occupational psychologists should be retained to make this adaptation.

Summary

Essentially there are three ways in which organizations can obtain and use reputable psychological tests:

- by their personnel or other staff attending training courses recognized by the British Psychological Society

- by retaining an occupational psychologist as an external consultant

- by employing an occupational psychologist or team of psychologists.

Any tests obtained by other means are unlikely to be effective, particularly as they will be administered, scored and interpreted by inadequately trained or completely untrained staff. Beware of the 'Barnum effect'. Remember too that tests which have been professionally developed overseas may require substantial work before being suitable for use in the UK.

5
Testing strategies

In this chapter, three aspects of testing strategy are discussed. First, there is the issue of how tests should be used: for example, they can be given at different stages of the selection procedure and they can be administered on a group or individual basis. Second, there is the issue of how tests should be presented, scored, etc. Finally, there is the issue of whether internal or external candidates should be treated in the same way. Each issue is now discussed in turn.

When to test

Tests can be given:

(i) as an aid to shortlisting

(ii) as part of the main selection procedure

(iii) as part of the detailed check on the final few

(iv) for development and other purposes

(i) Tests as an aid to shortlisting
Imagine a situation in which tests are used as part of the final selection procedure and in which a large proportion of the applicants are failing to reach the minimum standards required on the tests. If a test had been shown to be a valid predictor of subsequent success, there would be considerable savings in time and effort by using the test at an earlier stage in the selection process as a method of sifting; that is, applicants would be called in for testing alone and only those successful at the test would be

called back to the final selection procedure. This strategy is particularly useful if the final selection procedure is time consuming, since it reduces the costs incurred in seeing numbers of unsuitable candidates.

It may be possible to make even bigger savings by 'streamlining' the testing arrangements; for example, applicants might be brought to a central point to be tested in large groups by means of pencil and paper tests and in this way the cost of the administrator's time could be minimized. Under normal circumstances a single administrator can test about 20 people (for larger groups assistance is required) and advantage can sometimes be taken of low-cost rail and coach fares. Further savings can be made by using special answer sheets that can be quickly scored or even fed into a computer for scoring. A few major employers dealing with very large numbers may find it worthwhile to have tests administered on small business computers or computer terminals so that scoring can then take place automatically (see chapter 10).

Sifting procedures of this kind are in fact operated by major employers receiving large numbers of applications. Each year large organizations such as the Post Office receive several thousand applications from graduates seeking a career in management, and the decision as to which applicant to call to the main selection procedures (which may be an assessment centre lasting 24 hours) is partly based on the result of job related tests. A most radical sift is carried out by the Civil Service Commission who are faced with up to 10,000 applicants for as few as 200 vacancies for administration trainees; tests are used to reduce the number of candidates by 80 per cent or more, but some would regard this high level of dependence on tests as contentious.

However, four points need to be made about the use of tests as a means of shortlisting. The first is that when tests are used as a way of reducing large numbers there is often a temptation to control the number of applicants invited to the final selection by the simple method of raising or lowering the 'cut-off' or 'pass' mark without thinking through all the possible consequences. There are real dangers in this kind of *ad hoc* approach — if those with low marks are 'passed' they may be found to lack the abilities required to do the job, while restriction to those with only the highest marks may eliminate candidates with other strengths. This issue is discussed in more detail in chapter 8.

Secondly, tests are not the only method of shortlisting. Others include shortlisting on the basis of replies on standard or supplementary application forms and some organizations are now using 'bio-data', an approach in which numerical values are assigned to candidates' biographical replies according to research based on past applicants. For internal candidates, supervisors' reports can be another factor to take into account.

A third point about shortlisting is that there is sometimes scope for reducing numbers by giving more opportunity for self selection; in this way, the cost of testing and interviewing people who eventually find they do not want the job can be avoided. So, while it is the normal aim of an advertisement to attract as many applicants as possible, an advertisement for a job which is likely to be popular might also contain information about some of the less appealing aspects of the work, for example, the need to spend a lot of time away from home, or to be on call to deal with emergencies, or to work in difficult or unpleasant conditions.

When organizing and running selection procedures it is possible to calculate, or at least estimate, the ratios between the numbers attending the final selection procedure, the numbers offered appointments, the numbers accepting and the numbers actually starting. Shortlisting or self-selection requires an excess of applicants over the numbers that need to be called to the subsequent stages in the selection procedure. If there is no such excess there is a conflict between the use of shortlisting methods and filling all the vacancies. Under these circumstances there are a range of possible management strategies ranging from re-advertising to reviewing and adjusting the nature of the work and the working conditions (see also chapter 7).

(ii) Tests as part of the main selection procedure

There are several reasons why it could be desirable for tests to form part of the main selection procedure rather than be a separate part. First, separate testing may be considered unacceptable by candidates; this might be true if considerable travel was to be involved so that applicants might require a day's absence to attend testing and a further day to attend for interview.

A second reason for testing as part of the final procedure is that stock can then be taken of both the strengths and weaknesses of each candidate. However, if this is done some difficult decisions may have to be faced — for example a candidate with a number of past achievements may have a single indifferent test score and his/her potential for work at a higher level may therefore be questioned. Since test scores can sometimes be very good guides to potential it can be difficult to make the 'right' decision. Clearly a decision based on evidence from follow up studies of past selections would be preferable to an *ad hoc* decision (see chapter 9).

A third reason for testing being part of the final selection procedure could be to allow all internal candidates the opportunity to take part in the full assessment and thus to confirm an organization's interest in the development of its own staff whenever possible.

(iii) Tests as part of a detailed check on the 'final few'

Some organizations use tests as part of a final check on applicants rather than in a preliminary sift. There can be several reasons for this, including the fact that the final assessors may be senior staff from a head office or other location who have access to tests which are not available locally.

Sometimes consultant occupational psychologists (from within or outside the organization) are asked to advise at this late stage of selection and to use tests as part of their procedures. This strategy is of particular use when those involved in the earlier stages of selection are not accredited test users, when the most appropriate tests are available only to the psychologists, and/or when a view is required of how applicants compare with standards outside a particular organization. The individual assessment of candidates may also be preferred when there is a need for security about the vacancies and/or the individual applicants.

A final reason for delaying the involvement of experts until the end of the procedure is the view that their in-depth and sometimes expensive assessments should be confined to the most promising candidates only.

(iv) Testing for development and other purposes

Tests can be used not only for selection but also as an aid to helping employees with their career development. Tests can be used to help gauge suitability for specific vacancies or training opportunities (such as computer programming), or can be used as part of a process of helping individuals plan their career development by providing them with objective feedback about their abilities and aptitudes, personality values and interests.

There are two main ways in which tests can be used as an aid to career development. First, they can be used by an occupational psychologist or trained personnel manager working with just one individual; the individual being counselled may agree to take a variety of tests and questionnaires and may then be counselled about the results and the implications. Such work is demanding of the individual counsellor who needs to have a wide breadth and depth of knowledge both about tests and occupational information both within and outside the organization. However, such counselling can be carried out in confidence and at relatively short notice.

A second approach to career development which may involve tests is the assessment centre (see chapter 3). Initially, such centres were another form of selection, attempting to assess those individuals who had the attributes identified as being important in long term managerial success (Dulewicz 1982). In time, however, the emphasis has changed and many assessment centres are now much more orientated to helping individuals to achieve greater self awareness of their own strengths and weaknesses and subsequently making use of this information in planning their development. Assessment centres are administratively more complex and are therefore difficult to arrange at short notice. Participants are often required to work together and/or compete against each other, so that they often have the opportunity to assess their own performance with that of the other participants. Because assessment centres often involve several specially trained personnel and other managers with contrasting backgrounds and experience there can be a wide and informed view of opportunities within the organization.

Psychological tests may be used as part of the assessment centre programme in this context just as in the selection setting. Indeed, it is not unknown for them also to be used as a way of selecting people to go on to assessment centres. This reflects the fact that assessment centres are expensive and that not everyone can benefit from attending, so it makes sense for both individuals and organizations to try to ensure that only those who will get something from the experience go through it. Further, sifting can help to prevent people attending the centres who would find the procedures excessively demanding. So here, the use of tests in selection and in development come together.

Psychometric measures are given as an aid to self development in many other settings as well; typically, they are administered to managers on training courses so that they can see the results and have an opportunity to discuss the implications for their personal approach to work. Personality measures such as the Myers-Briggs Type Indicator, OPQ and Cattell 16PF are all frequently used in this way.

Finally, tests have been used as an aid to the development of teams as well as individuals. Belbin (1981) and others have shown how work groups, put together on the basis of the right mix of personality characteristics, can perform more effectively than randomly constituted groups, even when the latter are intellectually more able. So, for example, the ideal management team would not only have the appropriate skills in specialist terms (eg finance, operations, personnel, sales and marketing) but would also compliment each other in the way that they would work together at a particular problem.

Test administration

Testing procedures have become increasingly streamlined. Originally, many tests were administered individually, but in their place pencil and paper tests were used on a group basis because of the ease of administration. The latest development is that not only are some tests both administered and scored by computer, but also that the test items administered to individual candidates can be altered according to their speed of response and correctness of reply.

The capital outlay involved on computerized testing is considerable, but it does have attractions for major organizations handling large numbers of applicants each year (see chapter 10).

Testing internal and external applicants

There may be two arguments for adopting different policies towards internal and external candidates in terms of the tests to be taken and the scores to be considered acceptable. The first argument can arise when internal candidates already have experience bearing on the job for which they are applying, so that the amount of learning and adjustment they will need to make may appear to be small and it can be argued that assessments of performance on the related jobs may be a good guide to performance in the new job. In contrast, the demand on external candidates new to the organization may appear to be high. Accordingly, it might be proposed that testing should only be carried out on the external applicants. Alternatively, some differences may be allowed in the levels of test scores considered acceptable for each group. In deciding, much will depend on the ease or difficulty with which the transition has been made by past internal candidates and the confidence that can be placed in the assessments of performance. Account should also be taken of the likelihood of job experience affecting test scores. In particular, care should be taken that the procedure does not 'pass' internal candidates who lack the potential to develop further.

A second argument for treating each group differently is that there is a stronger case for providing internal candidates with 'feedback' as to how they got on in the selection procedure since it is important to sustain the motivation of employees who have been rejected. No doubt many external candidates would also like such feedback, particularly when they have taken a substantive test battery lasting several hours or even a day; they should be given it whenever possible (see chapter 8).

Summary

Test users often have a number of decisions to make about exactly how to make use of tests. The decisions include:

- whether, and at what stage, tests should be used for selection;

- whether, and at what stage, tests should be used for development;

- how tests should be administered and scored;

- whether internal and external candidates should be treated in the same way.

This chapter has addressed the pros and cons of various options. However, tests can be used in many different ways (Tyler and Miller 1986) and the final decision must be made according to specific circumstances.

6
Introducing tests
I Choosing the tests

This chapter considers how potential users should choose tests. While, for simplicity, it concentrates on the use of tests for selection, it should be borne in mind that:

- tests can be used as part of procedures for other purposes (eg career development, team building);

- tests can be used to help assess a very wide range of people and types and level of work, ranging from manufacturing to sales work and from trainees to managing directors.

Essential preliminaries

Before choosing tests it is important to have a clear idea of the range of qualities or characteristics required for successful job performance. This in turn depends on an appreciation of the work to be done. Details of the work to be done are normally collected together as a job description, while the qualities or characteristics required for successful job performance form a person specification. Selection methods, including tests, then have to be chosen. Each stage is discussed in turn.

Job descriptions
The main purpose of a job description for selection purposes is to identify the tasks and activities which are crucial to the successful job performance. From these details the qualities required in ideal applicants (the person specification) can be assessed by a deductive process. In addition, the job description should provide information about features of the work likely to attract (or even

deter) candidates, including hours of work, pay, etc. Such information can be circulated so that a degree of self-selection can occur.

It is rare to find comprehensive and up-to-date job descriptions waiting to be used for selection purposes and more often than not information has to be specially collected; this is traditionally done using a check list to cover salient features, such as the aims and objectives of the job, responsibilities, resources available and so on; it is normal too to involve current job holders, their bosses, etc, so as to build up a detailed picture.

In practice, the amount of detail to be collected will depend on the number of vacancies to be filled and the importance and complexity of the job. If the vacancy is important there are a number of special techniques which can be used to make sure that a comprehensive picture is obtained; examples of the main types of techniques, which can be used singly or in combination are as follows:

- *Interview:* using a structured process such as Flanagan's Critical Incident Technique, Kelly's Repertory Grid Technique, or perhaps internally developed structured questionnaires which have particular relevance to the type of work being done;

- *Job analysis questionnaires:* these have been developed as a result of extensive research and continuous modifications. Examples are McCormick's Position Analysis Questionnaire for lower level jobs, and an equivalent version for supervisory and management jobs;

- *Diary technique:* this involves the incumbent keeping a diary of his key activities over a long period.

The person specification:
As described earlier the person specification comprises a list of qualities to be sought in an ideal applicant; it is based on inferences made from the job description about the personal qualities required.

Again a check list approach can have an advantage in terms of helping to make sure that nothing important is missed. The most widely used framework in the UK is the late Professor Alec Rodger's Seven Point Plan (1953), which recommends specifying the characteristics required in the ideal applicant under seven headings:

1 Physical make-up

2 Attainments

3 General intelligence

4 Special aptitudes

5 Interests

6 Disposition (personality)

7 Circumstances (domestic, mobility, family traditions, etc).[1]

From the information collected in the job description, the person specification is deduced for each of the seven headings. For some jobs there may be requirements in terms of height and weight; entry requirements to the police service are often cited as an example. However, it should be noted that any arbitrary requirements may be challenged on the grounds of unfair discrimination — in America, for example, the height requirement for police officers is now based on the argument that they should be tall enough to aim a gun over the roof of a car while using the car as protection. Minimum requirements should be realistic and should relate to the demands of the job and behaviour required for successful performance.

In drawing up lists of this kind it is good practice to distinguish between essential and desirable characteristics; it is important not to have too many essentials or it may be impossible to find anyone who meets the specifications. Should this happen, matters will have to be resolved by, for example, relaxing some of the essential criteria, reviewing the pay or other benefits or even changing the way that the work is to be done (see also chapter 8).

When drawing up the person specification it can sometimes be helpful to identify any contra-indicators, that is features that may make some applicants unsuitable; for example, regular commitments in the local community would be a contra-indicator for a job

1 In the light of subsequent Equal Opportunities Legislation any questions should be confined to exploring job-related issues such as availability and mobility rather than circumstances *per se*.

involving frequent travel away from home, unless of course the applicant was prepared to change his or her lifestyle. However, in practice what matters is that the applicant is able to take on frequent travel away from home and not any other details of the candidate's life style.

When using check lists such as the seven point plan, it is normal to specify at least one characteristic under each heading. However, there will of course be differences in the types of quality sought according to the nature of the vacancy to be filled. For example, in the selection of a senior manager, some of the skills, abilities and personality characteristics on the following list might be considered important:

Oral communication skills

Written communication skills

Emotional adjustment

Analytical ability

Fertility of mind

Flexibility

Drive

Ascendancy

Planning and organization

Social skill

Delegation and control

Choosing the selection method

The next stage of the selection process is to choose the appropriate selection methods to assess the qualities considered to be important. Possibilites include:

Application forms

References and other written reports

Interviews (individual or panel)

Psychometric tests

Psychometric questionnaires

Group discussions, simulation exercises etc in which candidates
work together or compete with each other

In addition, self-selection among applicants is encouraged by
many organizations (see chapter 5).

A useful aid to choosing the appropriate methods is a matrix
with the methods down one side, and the requirements (eg the
headings from the Seven Point Plan) across the top. A tick is then
placed in the appropriate cell of the matrix for each method which
provides relevant information for each heading, ensuring that each
heading is covered by at least one method. It is preferable that
more than one method provides information about each requirement so that there is a cross check. Any inconsistencies can be
investigated through the interview by careful scrutiny of the
written data or by following up references if possible.

Tests and questionnaires are particularly valuable for assessing
intelligence and special aptitudes under the Seven Point Plan
framework, and for providing structured, quasi-objective data
about interests and disposition. Apart from assessment centres
(which often involve tests and questionnaires) the other methods
have shown very poor reliability and validity for assessing these
characteristics. In contrast, tests and questionnaires also have
some limitations as when, for example, collecting data on
availability for work or physical make-up.

Which test?
As noted in chapter 2, there are over 5,000 psychometric
instruments available in the English language alone. Even
restricting choice to those available to non-psychologists, potential
test users face a psychometric jungle, a jungle with more than its
fair share of predators! The route might be charted by three As:
(a) Availability (b) Appropriateness and (c) Acceptability.

(a) Availability
One obvious constraint on choice is the availability of tests, either
in terms of the organization having staff qualified to use them or in
terms of their being obtainable by non-psychologists at all (see
chapter 2). However, all the tests described in chapter 3 (and
many others) are potentially available providing that people have

been sent on the appropriate courses.

The restriction of supply to trained staff does mean that an organization considering using tests needs first to audit its own resources of staff who are trained in this area. Some staff may have been trained while working for other employers. Should there be few or none, then a decision has to be made on whether to invest in sending people on the relevant courses or to have a special course run for the organization (both of which may mean a certain amount of delay) or to bring in consultant occupational psychologists (see chapter 4).

(b) Appropriateness

Imagine that a personal specification has been drawn up listing, amongst other things, emotional stability and extroversion as desirable attributes for the person appointed. As the tests must be appropriate to assess these characteristics, the next stage is to survey what is available. It may turn out that there are a whole string of instruments purporting to measure these qualities of emotional stability and extroversion. How then can a decision be made as to which of them is best and most appropriate? Factors to consider include the following:

- Evidence of reliability

- Evidence of validity

- Evidence of the use of the test elsewhere

- Normative data

- Preventing unfair discrimination.

Evidence of reliability: The reliability of a test is a measure of its consistency (chapter 2). Any worthwhile test should be supported by evidence of this. It will normally be summarized in terms of a single figure ranging from 0 to +1, with 0 indicating a complete lack of reliability and +1 showing perfect reliability; if the figures were based on test-retest reliability, +1 would mean people getting exactly the same absolute or relative test scores on separate occasions (chapter 2). Perfect reliability is never achieved, but in ability tests reliability of +0.75 or above based on a sample size of at least 100, should be expected.

Measures of personality are subject to rather greater variation, which is understandable as the expression of personality is perhaps more susceptible to transient influence than is the demonstration of ability when individuals are doing their best to perform well on tests. For personality measures, a reliability of +0.65 or above based on a sample size of 100 may be considered acceptable.

Evidence of validity: Validity measurements are evidence about whether the test is measuring what it purports to measure and different kinds of validity were outlined in chapter 2. The measurement can be illustrated by the extent to which a test has demonstrated that it relates to some external criterion as, for example, tests given to bank clerks might relate to their subsequent job performance. Again, as in the case of reliability, the evidence is likely to be summarized in the form of a validity co-efficient that ranges from -1 to $+1$. A correlation of $+1$ means that on a graph plotting test score against job performance for a number of individuals there would be a linear relationship between test scores and performance so that the person with the highest test score has the highest job performance. This is illustrated in Figure 1.

Figure 1

A graph showing a correlation of $+1$ between test scores and job performance. Each cross represents the test score/job performance for one individual; for simplicity only five individuals are represented.

A correlation of -1 would mean that the person with the lowest test score had the highest performance. A correlation of 0 would mean that there is no relationship between the scores and job performance.

Test manuals should contain data about validity. For example, the manual for a numerical reasoning test might show that for a sample of people selected for the job of bank clerk the test scores correlated +0.35 with the ratings of performance made on those same people by their supervisors one year later; this would mean that there was a tendency for those scoring well on the test to perform well, but prediction would be far from certain.

The size of validity correlations quoted in manuals may at first sight seem low but there are plenty of reasons, some of which are dealt with below, why it is unrealistic to expect high ones. For various technical reasons it is difficult to specify precisely what is and is not acceptable in terms of validity co-efficients; under some circumstances, validities as low as +0.10 might make worthwhile improvements to the effectiveness of selection although correlations of +0.50 might be an initial target and +0.20 a realistic goal. Remember too that results from tests are often used in combination because successful job applicants need to be competent in several different ways. For example, an applicant for a clerical job might need to be competent at numerical calculations, understanding the meaning of words, filing, and carrying out simple instructions using tables of information; the four relevant tests might individually have rather low predictive power but together might reach an altogether more useful level.

Whenever looking at validity information in test manuals, check the size of the samples involved in the validity study as well as the correlation itself (see below).

Table 1

Test Score	Number of promotions gained in first four years			
	0 (%)	1 (%)	2 (%)	
51–60	60	30	10	(100%)
61–70	40	35	25	(100%)
71+	25	35	40	(100%)

People who find it difficult to understand the implications of validity may find the hypothetical example in table 1 helpful. Imagine that a test has been given to help select for a job. The test results are being validated by comparing the test scores with the number of promotions of each individual during the first four years. The table shows the percentage of people who achieved 0, 1 or 2 promotions during that period.

In the example, 40 per cent of the candidates who obtain a test score of 71 or above go on to achieve two promotions in the next four years, compared with just 10 per cent of those who had test scores in the 51−60 range; increases in test scores seem to be clearly predictive of career success over the period examined. However, given just one test score, it can be seen that the table is by no means a perfect guide to the probable success of the individual with that score.

Validity evidence often has two components, the test score and the measure of performance (or criterion measurement). A wide range of criterion measures may be utilized, ranging from specific measures of task performance to rather broader indicators of success like performance appraisal ratings, salary increases and promotions. None of these criteria are themselves perfect measures of performance. The promotion system in the organization will not be 100 per cent accurate in identifying those most deserving of advancement, partly because in many cases the appraisal process to which it is linked is subject to all sorts of biases and imperfections. Thus, using either promotions gained or appraisal ratings as the criteria by which the effectiveness of tests is judged is never going to yield a wholly accurate assessment of how good a test actually is.

Even when objective measures of performance are available, as in the case of many sales jobs, they seldom tell the whole story; the sales made have to be interpreted against the background of the potential of the territory, the competition, the manner in which the results were achieved (have claims or promises been made that will prove difficult to live up to and hence make selling in that area more difficult next year?), and so on. But whatever their deficiencies, criteria of the kinds mentioned here are the best that are usually available and are certainly far, far better than no validation evidence at all.

Occasionally, test users may be faced with several alternative tests each with similar availability, reliability and validity. How then may a choice be made?

Under such circumstances, a decision may rest on the precise reason for requiring the tests. For example, if the primary purpose for testing is to assess suitability for a particular job, the ideal kind of validity evidence to be sought from the manuals of the test under consideration will be that they have shown an acceptable level of correlation with some form of performance rating or other measures in identical work. However, beware of deciding that work is 'identical' simply because a common job title is used (see chapter 2) and be prepared to take professsional advice since differences may significantly affect the worth of the tests.

Where the aim of testing is wider, and the concern is to predict performance over a number of jobs that an individual might do in the first couple of years and possibly to give some indication of career potential, the prospective test user should seek evidence of correlations with performance measures over a period of time and with indices of progress (salary growth, number of promotions etc).

The question, then, is whether the test has been shown to predict the outcome required. That said, however, the imperfections of each of the various performance criteria used are such that the more validation evidence there is, preferably including a range of criterion measures, the better.

Evidence of the use of the test elsewhere: Although it is important to know whether proper validation studies have been carried out, such studies are rare because of the sample sizes needed and the time and experience required. But while there may not be a wealth of validity data, the tests may be widely used and there may be considerable information about their use and acceptability which could influence a decision about whether or not to use the tests in particular circumstances.

Enquiries to the test publishers, to consultant occupational psychologists, to experienced users and reference to books and other publications describing test usage (eg Miller, 1975), can therefore be useful. Some of the information may be positive — for example, major companies may comment favourably about the worth of the tests, about the ease of administration and scoring and so on. Conversely, the information may be negative — for example, applicants elsewhere may be failing to understand instructions, test booklets may be found to have pages missing or to be poorly printed, and so on.

Finding that a test or series of tests have been adopted widely means that if they are given in the selection context, there is always the chance that candidates will have encountered them before. Indeed, since people tend to apply for more than one job at the same time, it is not at all uncommon to find candidates taking some of the same tests for different organizations in selection procedures just a few days apart. This inevitably carries the danger of familiarity breeding enhanced performance; for example, on the second and third presentations of an ability test candidates are likely to get marginally higher scores, but may not improve further thereafter; however exceptions have been noticed and test manuals should ideally give information on this point. In those instances where the individual has also been provided with feedback on the results of a previous assessment, this may considerably affect the attitude to encountering the same tests again; personality measures may be particularly subject to distortion where the person feels the need to try to modify the picture that emerged last time.

Very widespread use of a test does carry with it this problem, and ideally test publishers should provide information on the effects of previous testing both with and without feedback of results. Alternatively, users might aim to compile their own information. But at present if equally good but less frequently used measures are available it may be worth opting for them. Either way, it is good practice to check whether candidates have been through any similar procedures recently and if they have, what tests were involved (they may not know the names, but the descriptions given will often give a good clue as to the identity). This sometimes allows users either to change the tests to be given or at least to be aware of some possible effect of prior experience. Unless the previous testing session was very recent, in the last week or two, it is unlikely that scores on ability tests will be significantly affected.

Normative design: The use of a test elsewhere does, however, have advantages. It is of litle value to know that someone has achieved a score of 56 on a test, where possible range of scores is 10 to 75, without knowing how others compare with this individual's score on the test. In other words, normative data is required (see chapter 2). An important factor in choosing tests is whether or not they can provide normative data relevant to particular needs. For example, an organization selecting school leavers for clerical jobs may want tests of numerical calculation and verbal ability that have normative data for 16 year olds who have been entered for the highest GCSE grades; there would be little point in judging the school leavers scores by comparing them with the performance of graduates on the same tests.

Problems of some complexity can arise because abilities can influence career decisions and people tend to stop studying subjects in which they are making little progress. Imagine an engineering company assessing candidates for jobs in technical sales. Direct comparisons of candidates with an engineering or technical background with those of people who had a predominantly arts background might not aid a sound decision since as a group the latter would probably do significantly better on verbal and significantly worse on numerical or spatial ability measures than the engineers. Over and above the test scores judgements would need to be made about the speed with which non-technical people might pick up technical knowledge, and the extent to which technical people might develop verbal sales skills. The availability of suitable training might be a key factor.

As far as possible, choose tests with norms that allow the comparison of like with like; the norms should also be based on samples that are large enough to give confidence that they are representative (at least 100 and preferably 200 or more). The manual that accompanies the test should contain that information. While it is possible, and desirable, for an organization eventually to build up its own norms, this clearly takes some time.

Unfair discrimination: Another important standard by which to assess the suitability of any test is whether its use is consistent with equal opportunities legislation.

Ideally, tests should be developed so that they do not discriminate unfairly. Unfortunately it is very difficult to produce 'culture-fair' tests, as they have come to be known. It is generally acknowledged that every individual's environmental and cultural background will affect his/her test performance. The greater the variance between the individual's background and the norm for the culture in which the tests have been developed and used, the greater the possible unfair discrimination.

When choosing a test, check the manual to see whether the test performance of sub groups (eg men and women or ethnic minorities) has been investigated and documented. If this evidence is available and indicates that the test does not discriminate unfairly, this can be regarded as a positive feature. However, it should not lead to complacency: always continue to check for the possibility of unfair discrimination when monitoring its subsequent use.

If relevant evidence is not available in the manual (as is almost certain to be the case for tests developed before the mid 1970s) or is unfavourable, this does not mean that the test cannot be used: rather the situation should be monitored very carefully and corrective action taken if necessary, eg change to a different test.

Given a situation in which tests may discriminate unfairly against individuals from different backgrounds, there are several practical points to be considered when choosing tests which will help to make them more acceptable to candidates and less likely to discriminate unfairly.

- Ensure that both the content of the test and the instructions are directly relevant to the job being selected for. For example, the use of tests with complex written instructions cannot be justified in selection for a job which does not require individuals to follow complex written instructions. In such a case the tests are also likely to discriminate unfairly against those whose command of the English language is sufficient to do the job, but not to understand the test instructions.

- Provide test description handouts or example sheets, which describe the tests and the reasons for using them, and give example questions for applicants to try; these steps have been found to increase acceptability and reduce unfair discrimination. When choosing a test, check whether these are available from the supplier. If not, check that the publisher is agreeable to their production locally.

- Ensure that the tests under consideration contain examples for the candidate to try before they start the test. Candidates from some ethnic groups or social classes may well be more apprehensive when faced with tests. Untimed example sessions at the start of a test can help to get rid of nerves and unfamiliarity, thus allowing everyone to start the proper test on a more equal footing.

Test description handouts and untimed example sessions are useful not only for avoiding unfair discrimination against groups who are accepted as traditionally disadvantaged (ethnic minorities, women, disabled) but also for equalizing different degrees of test 'sophistication' in an apparently homogeneous group.

Tests are only part of a selection procedure, and the rest of the procedure should also be scrutinized to make sure that unfair discrimination is avoided (see chapters 9 and 10).

(c) Acceptability

Having run through some of the main aspects of judging the appropriateness of tests, it is time to consider the final element in the choice of process. This concerns the acceptability of the measures adopted to those being assessed. Factors to be considered include (i) the presentation of the test material (ii) the face validity of the tests and (iii) the acceptability of the test items.

The general presentation of the test items: Poorly produced, dog-eared or drab test booklets do not endear themselves to candidates nor inspire confidence among clients or other managers. Appearance should therefore be a factor in choice.

More important, however, is the apparent nature of the tests themselves. What are the people being tested likely to think the tests are for? How will they feel about what they are being asked to do or say?

Face validity: The extent to which a test looks as though it is measuring what it sets out to measure (see chapter 2). Whether it looks the part or not is actually a very unreliable guide as to the real, criterion-related validity of a test. But face validity does matter in other ways. With ability tests, there is little problem, since the type of intellectual ability being assessed is usually fairly obvious and knowing it will make scant difference to anyone's performance. Also, the rationale for giving ability tests is perhaps more readily (but by no means universally) accepted by candidates than is the rationale for personality measures. It is here that most of the trouble arises.

Developing personality questionnaires that have high face validity reduces the danger of alienating the individual being assessed. Such alienation might well have happened when applicants for normal managerial posts were asked to complete a personality inventory, much used in the USA, which included questions about bowel movements. Applicants might reasonably have wondered what on earth this was supposed to be assessing and what relevance it had to the job in question; they might become increasingly annoyed at such an intrusive and seemingly irrelevant line of questioning, to the extent that a gut feel of quite another kind would be telling them that this is not the kind of organization in which they wish to work.

There are of course two problems here. One is the obscure purpose of the exercise and the other is the unacceptable nature of particular questionnaire items. Unfortunately, they interact with each other to produce a potentially unfavourable response. It is possible to construct personality inventories that are much more transparent and which thus are more likely to have higher face validity. People can see what is being measured and can relate it to the purpose of the assessment. In addition, such readily understandable measures are easier to use in any subsequent feedback session. Unfortunately, it also means that the candidates are in a better position to try to manipulate the impression they give of themselves on such measures; it potentially helps them to fake.

Turning to the problem of personality inventory items that may seem bizarre or extreme in some way, these are usually present as elements in scales that tap aspects of emotional adjustment, or maladjustment to be more accurate. Or they may have the purpose of picking up people who are at the outer limits of some personality dimension (which again may have implications about the individual's adjustment in a more restricted sense). If personality measures are employed which avoid the use of such items, then it will probably be at the cost of not assessing these aspects of the person as well as they might have done. Incidentally, it should be pointed out here that some people do endorse extreme items of this kind; they do not always see them as being odd and do not cover-up (though equally obviously, some do!).

Opinion is divided about the best way forward, some taking the view that the candidate's self knowledge is helpful, others distrusting it because they fear that some candidates will manipulate their replies. Accordingly many procedures seek both to assess candidates and to give them the opportunity to report assessments of themselves; some go further and also ask the candidates to assess each other.

If a choice is to be made it should reflect particular circumstances. If it is of particular concern that those selected be emotionally resilient, because the jobs concerned are high-stress, then the balance may be felt to tip in favour of using measures that may be a little lower in acceptability to the candidate. In other circumstances, as when there is strong competition to recruit the best candidates, it might be felt that while there is still a need to assess them, it should not be done in such a fashion that it drives them into the arms of the competitors.

Acceptability: consider how tests will appear to candidates. For example, when choosing personality measures, the sensible thing to do is to go through the inventories and reflect on how they will seem to the candidates. Even if it is felt to be essential to use questionnaires that ask some of the more extreme types of question, there is still a great deal that can be done to minimize any adverse reactions; this is discussed later in this book (administration of tests and feedback of results).

Finally, under the heading of Acceptability, the use of *micro-computers* in testing needs to be considered. This is discussed in detail in chapter 10.

Summary

Whether or not to choose tests should be based on the following:

- the nature of the work to be done;
- an analysis of the characteristics of ideal applicants;
- a review of other possible selection methods.

If tests are to be used, choice should be based on:

- availability
- appropriateness, including
    reliability
    validity
    the use of the test elsewhere
    normative data
    avoiding unfair discrimination
- acceptability, including
    face validity
    the acceptability of individual items.

7
Introducing tests
11 Planning and implementation

This chapter deals with four issues: getting agreement to proceed with testing; organizing testing; maintaining a large-scale testing programme; and testing individuals.

Getting agreement to proceed with testing

Assume that a stage has been reached where a strong case can be made for the use of tests as part of a procedure for the selection of graduate entrants (broadly similar principles would apply if other groups were to be involved). The recommendation to use tests could be based on a number of points including the following:

- a follow-up of some recent graduate entrants in your organization has shown that some have given up because of pressure of work while others have been given poor reports at the end of induction training and at the end of their first year of employment;

- an analysis of the work done by graduate entrants has been carried out and the qualities and skills required for successful job performance has been identified; from these analyses possible tests have been identified;

- the manuals for the tests show 'good' evidence of the worth of the tests for graduate selection, viz sample sizes have been over 100 and reliability and validity estimates have been satisfactory (see chapter 9);

- the tests you want to use are similar to those used by other companies selecting graduates and to those used by your major competitors who do not seem to be facing the level of 'wastage' problems that your organization is facing.

A recommendation that tests should be introduced as part of the selection procedure based on the above information may appear water-tight. However, it is important to be aware of some of the reasons why proposals to use tests may not be supported or may even meet resistance:

- the number of applicants and the number of vacancies may not seem to others to justify the costs of staff being trained to use tests; under these circumstances the case for using tests should be carefully costed and alternative strategies should be considered, such as the retention of a consultant or sharing the cost of selection with other companies through a group scheme;

- questions may be raised about the fairness of tests, *vis à vis* applicants from ethnic minorities, those who do not match the prevailing sexual stereotype for the vacancy, and the disabled; such questions may be anticipated if it is proposed to use tests for selection in organizations keen to advance opportunities for minority groups, and careful background research with the test developers and publishers may be required to establish the fairness of the proposed procedures;

- the judgement that the use of tests will be beneficial may be challenged; until the tests have actually been used in a particular organization and results followed up, it is impossible to demonstrate the worth of tests with absolute certainty and some may exploit this weakness in the case being put forward; explanations involving probability and other statistics may impress some but infuriate others. For example, people who failed the 11 plus, whose sons and daughters failed the 11 plus or those who feel that they were inappropriately placed during wartime or national service may be strongly opposed to testing. In contrast, others may be supportive because of their past successes in selections involving tests, or because they have found career guidance involving tests useful for their children etc.

- Some may fear the consequences of better selection; for example, trainers may be concerned that courses may not be filled if higher selection standards are applied, while supervisors may fear the appointment of bright subordinates whom they will find difficult to manage.

So even if a case is technically sound there is no guarantee of proposals being accepted. Therefore some time should be spent seeking the views of those who may influence the decision and making sure the proposals embrace the points to which they are likely to be sympathetic and deal effectively with any objections. If written proposals are also to be presented orally it may be worth holding back a little information about the potential worth of tests in order to strengthen the case being made on the day.

Sometimes it is impossible to make a strong case, as when no proven tests exist for the type of vacancy to be filled. Resistance can also be strong for this or other reasons. One way forward can then be to get agreement to a trial in which the tests are administered at the time of selection but the results are not used. Later the test scores can be compared with performance as in a predictive validation study (see chapter 9) and a decision about whether or not to use the tests for selection can be based on the results.

Organizing testing

Assume that proposals for the testing of graduate entrants have been approved. A training course in the use of tests has been successfully completed (or the services of an occupational psychologist retained) and it has been decided to use the tests as part of an initial sift — that is, only those shortlisted applicants who reach a satisfactory standard on the test will be invited to the final interviews. What preparations are necessary?

First, thought needs to be given to likely response, offer and appointment rates. Precise numbers and types of vacancy can be difficult to forecast and may change at short notice according to the latest business plans for expansion or contraction, changes in turnover rates etc. In addition, when recruiting graduate entrants there is the problem of estimating how many of those accepting offers will actually start work and not withdraw their acceptance if a better offer arises. Such problems are rarely appreciated by applicants who are understandably annoyed if they reply promptly to advertisements only to find that all vacancies have been filled. They are particularly annoyed if they are successful during the initial part of a selection procedure and then find out that all the vacancies are filled before they have the opportunity to attend the final part.

Whatever the difficulties in making accurate forecasts, administrators must persevere with the best estimates available and try to avoid major errors. For example, there is little point in inviting all applicants for initial tests if it will be impossible to interview all who are successful. On the other hand, if the number of initial applicants is too low and the numbers are then reduced because of the use of tests, the numbers being passed on to final interview may be insufficient. Past records may help to judge the numbers that should ideally be attracted, as may advice on the current state of affairs from careers officers, business contracts, advertising agencies, etc. It may be necessary to use suitable application forms (or design a supplement to an existing form) in order to sift on other relevant grounds if need be.

Applicants should be told in advance what the selection procedure will involve — perhaps in the job advertisement, but certainly when sending out application forms and job descriptions in response to enquiries. Ideally applicants should be sent handouts ahead of the procedure which outline the kinds of tests to be used and give one or two example items for practice; they will then have time to seek further information from public libraries, from relatives and friends etc. The handouts should also describe the selection procedure as a whole and answer any questions commonly raised by applicants. Applicants should be warned to bring spectacles and hearing aids if they need them. Major employers such as the Post Office have printed leaflets for use in major recruitment programmes.

Testing should be carried out in groups of appropriate size; a test administrator should not normally test more than 20 people without assistance from other staff, though the precise number would depend on (i) the level of appointment and type of test being used; (ii) environmental factors, such as room size, and (iii) the testing materials available.

(i) *Level of appointment and type of test:* a few applicants can feel threatened by some kinds of testing — an example might be an applicant for a top management post who has never seen a personality questionnaire but who has heard criticisms from others; if testing is being carried out in circumstances in which good applicants are scarce, testing candidates individually or in pairs so that they can be personally greeted and given some individual attention is preferable to testing in larger groups in which individuals may feel anonymous.

(ii)   *Environmental factors:*   among the factors to be considered are:

the size of the room

adequate lighting

acoustics

quiet and free from interruption

comfortable seating

suitable work surface on which to rest test papers etc

appropriate heating and ventilation

(iii) *The testing materials available:*   some tests comprise question booklets and separate answer sheets which enables the relatively expensive question booklets to be reused; the cost and availability of the booklets may influence the numbers to be tested at any single time.

Times for testing should relate to public transport times; consider late afternoon or evening sessions for those still studying; avoid clashes with examination dates. Check that there will not be any disruptions during testing, such as fire drills or major repairs in or near the building.

Make sure that applicants will be properly received and that there are suitable refreshment and toilet facilities.

Have applicants confirm their attendance — allow time for this and specify a contact point within the organization.

As an introduction to the testing session, briefing about the use of tests should be repeated and expanded as part of the essential process of settling the candidate down. People generally feel more at ease and in control of a situation when they know what is going to happen and when; this applies to testing as much as to anything else, and it is important to continue to work to overcome any anxiety that individuals may feel when faced with psychological tests. Indeed, the selection of those who are to be handling the test sessions should focus among other things on the ability of the people concerned to establish rapport with the candidates and to deal with them in a sensitive and socially skilled way (see chapter 2).

Reputable tests have detailed instructions on administration and these must be followed exactly. If the test instructions have to be read out to the candidates, the test administrator chosen must have a suitably clear and loud voice. If the testing session is a long one, time should be allowed for natural breaks.

If tests are being used as a sift, allow a sufficient period between testing and the final stage of selection for the tests to be marked and for those who are successful to be called forward: prior warning of the dates for the final stage of selection can allow the candidates to pencil the dates in their diaries.

Records should be kept of all test scores (preferably the answer sheets as well) to facilitate follow-up studies to check the worth of the tests and of the procedure as a whole.

Maintaining a large-scale testing programme

Some organizations use tests on a large scale. For example, Post Office Psychological Services supply up to 40,000 tests annually to over 200 locations throughout the UK.

When providing tests for use in decentralized organizations, instructions have to be issued on all the above points and staff trained. The following points also have to be considered:

- the supply of tests from a central point; if this is done, stock control and distribution systems have to be implemented;

- facilities for handling enquiries have to be established; for example, there may be enquiries from staff who need to administer tests and who have yet to attend formal training programmes;

- there need to be systems for monitoring and inspecting the operation to ensure that good testing practices are being followed; steps will need to be taken to ensure that test materials are kept secure, samples of used test materials will need to be checked to make sure that they have been correctly scored, etc.

The following are illustrative of the kinds of problems that can arise in any large-scale testing operations:

- recommended tests may not be given (eg shortage of time, not considered suitable by local staff, fear that applicants may be put off by testing);

- other tests may be added or substituted, (again both suitability and/or time required may be questioned by local staff);

- inappropriate norms may be used for grading;

- confusion may have arisen over pass marks (eg when instructions stating that 'grade 4 is a pass' are interpreted by some to imply that all those obtaining any other grade should be rejected);

- local standards have been varied (lowered to fill vacancies or increased to keep numbers of applicants down) without regard to the requirements of the job and the future prospects for staff who are selected (see chapters 5 and 8);

- senior managers without training in the use of the tests may demand unsupervised access to test materials and to test scores; some may even wish to keep records of the scores for further reference, with plans to look at the test scores when reviewing the performance of subordinates or even plans to evaluate the worth of the tests;

- staff whose work involves the use of tests may fail to master their administration and interpretation, and may be unable to convince local managers of the need to follow recommended procedures;

- test materials may not be returned when the testing staff move to other work; left unattended they may become compromised.

Testing individuals

There are a number of possible reasons for giving tests to an individual; for example, the individuals may be applicants for top management posts, or even people from widely differing levels and backgrounds whose placement in the organization may not be working out.

To promote as positive an attitude as possible on the part of those tested, it helps to foster a co-operative or collaborative perspective on the exercise; and it assists greatly if a confidential feedback session on the results can be offered, so that there is something in it for the individual (see chapter 9). If appropriate, it can be worth pointing out that selecting people who are wrong for a job or who are not going to perform satisfactorily is probably not going to do them any favours in the long run.

Summary

Even if the case for introducing testing is technically sound, proposals to do so may be resisted. Accordingly the case for testing must be prepared carefully and 'sold' to others who may also influence the decision.

Other factors affecting the success of testing range from winning the co-operation and interest of individual applicants to making sound administrative arrangements for larger groups. The choice of a suitable person to do the testing is particularly important (see chapter 4).

8
Introducing tests
III Making and communicating decisions

Because of the vast number of tests available it is impossible to give detailed advice on the interpretation of scores on particular tests. What is possible is to give some basic principles that guide the use of test information in decision making. They are:

- using 'cut-offs';

- using profiles;

- combining test results to increase predictive power;

- the integration of test results with other parts of the selection;

- access to test results; and

- giving feedback on test results.

Using 'cut-offs'

Pencil and paper aptitude tests can be administered to groups of applicants. For this reason they are often given at an early stage in the selection process as an aid to 'sifting' the applicants and deciding which should be called to interviews or other stages of the procedure which are more time consuming (see chapter 5).

Used wisely, the strategy can have considerable commercial significance. For example, the use of tests as part of an initial sifting sometimes enables the Post Office to appoint one in every four applicants that it assesses in depth for executive posts; however, when sifting has not been possible, the proportion appointed can fall dramatically and occasionally senior staff have spent days interviewing unsuitable candidates and not making any appointments.

In order to sift, 'cut-off' points need to be established on the test or tests that are being used. This section describes how 'cut-offs' can be set and discusses some possible disadvantages of this strategy.

To illustrate the point, imagine that an employer is faced with a large number of applicants for a two-year youth training scheme in engineering. In order to sift fairly and minimize the chances of failure during training, the work is studied and a decision made to use a test of mechanical aptitude. It is agreed that a personnel manager should attend a training course in the use of such a test.

While attending the training course, the personnel manager is given the information in table 2. Possible scores on the test range from 0 to 30, and based on a total sample (n) of 200 YTS applicants to four other employers the percentile ranks have been drawn up. (An individual's percentile score shows the percentage of applicants whose scores that individual has exceeded.)

Table 2

Mechanical Aptitude Test Score	Percentile rank for applicant
30	95+
28–29	90
25–27	80
21–24	70
16–20	60
12–15	50
8–11	40
7	30
6	20
3–5	10
0–2	5

There are at least five ways in which the personnel manager may decide on a 'cut-off' for sifting in his or her own organization:

- the first option is to press the test publishers for additional information about the use of the test elsewhere; this may yield recent information about the worth of the test being established for similar purposes;

- second, it may be possible to get relevant information from local business contacts through Institute of Personnel Management meetings etc; staff of local colleges involved in training may know of other companies using the same test; of course, if the test is used widely among local employers, its effectiveness could be reduced through applicants taking it several times and becoming practised (see chapter 6).

- third, it may be possible to test existing trainees whose performance is known; it is of course necessary to reassure those trainees that the test results would only be used as an aid to designing future selection procedures and will not affect their prospects; a potential problem here is that the existing trainees will not be as strongly motivated as they were at the time of selection and this may affect their test scores; further, the exercise will at best be a measure of concurrent rather than predictive validity (see chapter 2);

- fourth, a pragmatic decision could be made based on the numbers that can be accommodated in the final stages of selection and the likely final selection ratio; for example, it may be anticipated that one in six of those interviewed will be made job offers and that three of every five offered jobs will accept; the numbers to be 'passed' can then be calculated once all the applicants have been tested;

- fifth, the test could be given to applicants without the results being taken into account initially; selection could take place on other grounds and then the progress of applicants followed up to see whether there is a relationship between test scores and performance and whether a 'cut-off' can be established; while this approach has the advantage of providing information about what happens to applicants with low test scores, attitudes to this strategy will vary; some may welcome an objective trial but others may not be happy with the idea of taking on low scorers and waiting to see if they fail!

The actual method chosen will depend on circumstances. Factors to be taken into account include the following:

- what numbers of applicants and vacancies exist? With 1,000 applicants and 100 vacancies the worth of the test can be checked on the intake for a single year; with 10 applicants and one vacancy decisions will have to be based on the experience of test designers and others;
- how effective are present selection methods? If they are good it may be possible to let things run while the worth of the test is established; however, if urgent action is required arbitrary decisions may be necessary in the hope of improving the situation quickly;
- how many applicants are coming forward? Can the numbers be increased? If there are many vacancies and few applicants, the use of tests as a sift may make recruitment even more difficult;
- can a minimum standard be established below which applicants are unlikely to succeed?
- can a maximum score be established above which applicants may be too able and present problems because they are bored?

Mention has been made of the possibility of following up performance of those already recruited; in order to build up numbers this might involve data about the recruitment of employees over several years, but care must be taken in doing this; for example, if the standards of performance expected of

Table 3

Mechanical aptitude Test scores	Percentage of entrants completing training
25 and over	95
21–24	93
16–20	86
12–15	82
8–11	75
6–7	68
5 and below	45

employees has changed radically over recent years, it would not be appropriate to include all performance ratings. Returning to the earlier example about youth trainees, imagine that the data in table 3 was collected about the trainees who had taken the mechanical aptitude test, at the end of of the two-year training. Given the above data, the cut-off might ideally be set at the score of 25, so that the chance of those selected finishing their training would be 95 per cent. However, this strategy would mean creaming off the very best of the applicants in terms of test scores, and it is imporant to check whether there are sufficient applicants to make this a practical proposition.

In this example, the need to check is confirmed by looking back to table 2. Taking only those who scored 25 and above would mean selecting the top 20 per cent of applicants, so to find 20 people who attained this level of performance on the test a pool of 100 candidates would be needed. Sometimes the term 'selection' ratio is used to summarise the situation. If only those scoring above 25 were taken on there would be a selection ratio of 0.20 (the ratio of the number to be taken on, 20, to the number of applicants, 100).

But what if there are fewer than 100 applicants? One possible way to fill the vacancies will be to reduce the cut-off score. Thus, if there are only 50 applicants and 20 trainees are again required, the selection ratio would be 20:50 or 0.40 as it would normally be expressed. To recruit 20 trainees from 50 applicants would mean that the crucial test score would be lowered to 16, as it can be seen that 59 per cent of applicants get a score of 15 or below, and 40 per cent get 16 or above. Going back to the data on the relationship between test scores and completion of training, the proportion of applicants getting a score of 16 or more that would be expected to finish the training would be 86 per cent.

In practice the cut-off score would have to be lowered still further to allow for the rejection of candidates who are unsuitable in other parts of the selection procedure. Although tests can be the most useful part of a selection procedure they should never be used alone.

Sometimes the need to fill vacancies may lower the pass mark to a level where the likely percentage of failures will be unacceptable. One way of dealing with such circumstances is to put additional effort into the raising of the numbers of applicants by, for example, more advertising; other alternatives might be to improve induction and other training, to redesign the work to make it less demanding, etc.

In contrast, some employers are currently faced with the problem of having large numbers of well qualified people applying for relatively undemanding jobs. In the absence of data showing a clear statistical relationship between scores and the criterion, such employers sometimes assume that 'you can't have too much of a good thing' and cut-off points are raised higher and higher. However, the assumption does not always hold; for example, several studies have shown that managerial performance correlates with intellectual test scores only up to a point; beyond this point, very high test scores do not seem to be associated with superior managerial effectiveness.

Quite apart from this kind of finding, the blind pursuit of high test scores may simply result in the selection of a group of people who are over-qualified for the job in question, and who will quickly become frustrated, bored or dissatisfied and are then likely to leave.

Although examples given so far have been based on aptitude tests, the same issues apply when considering personality questionnaire results. Suppose, for instance, that a personality questionnaire has an emotionality scale. It may be desirable to set up a cut-off below which applicants are screened out as being anxiety prone or unstable. But what about people who score at the other extreme of the dimension? They may be very cold, unfeeling individuals who are inclined to ignore or to be unaware of the emotional reactions of others, and who may thus be highly insensistive. An organization will probably not want too many of that sort of person around, and certainly not in some jobs. Here, as in the case of ability tests, the use of a single cut-off point can over-simplify the situation.

Using profiles

Scores on personality inventories are often put together to produce a profile chart which shows the individuals position on each dimension in relation to the average score and in terms of the distribution of scores as a whole. This is a very popular way of summarizing the basic facts. The background against which the person's score is portrayed may be the norms built up for that organization or they may be the norms as supplied by the test producer in the test manual. Sometimes, as in Cattell's 16PF, the well known personality questionnaire, there is quite a range of profiles available showing the score patterns for different occupational groups.

The profiles appear so convenient and helpful that it is easy to overlook some important considerations in using them. The first is that to be of any real worth, the norms presented in the profile must be based on adequate sample sizes; groups of 40 or so are just not enough to be confident in the stability of the data; groups of at least 100 are essential and groups of 200 or more are to be preferred.

The second danger is that the norms used may not be appropriate. For example, it might be most appropriate to compare graduate applicants for general management with each other and/or applicants 12 months earlier; to compare them either with those actually taken on 12 months earlier or with graduates applying for sales posts could severely mislead.

The third danger is of thinking that the profile represents a picture of what is desirable and effective in terms of personal qualities for that group rather than simply what is typical. Profiles from groups of scientific researchers can illustrate that this is unwise. On the 16PF, these groups can be characterized by, amongst other things, tender mindedness (or emotional sensitivity). But in studies which have focused on an index of effectiveness, in this instance the number of publications the scientist produces, it has been found that the more effective members of this group are actually characterized by tough mindedness.

What occupational group profiles present is a picture of what is typical of people who have stayed in a particular job and perhaps adjusted to it. However, their experiences of the job might well have affected replies and hence their profiles. So one problem is that group profiles reflect concurrent validity rather than the preferable predictive validity (see chapter 2). Further, group profiles often do not differentiate between those in the group who are performing well and those who are not. It is of course possible to develop separate profiles for the successful and unsuccessful sub-groups and this more detailed information is required for effective selection decisions.

Combining test results to increase predictive power

The complexity of most jobs makes it unlikely that a single quality will determine success and therefore that a single test will be adequate to assess applicants' suitability. The question then arises of how to combine tests together into a battery. One way is to use multiple cut-offs, so that the tests are taken in a series, with only those individuals who have exceeded the critical score on the first test going on to take the second and so on. In practice this is a rather cumbersome process and is only likely to be used in a limited range of circumstances (generally where there is a multiple stage screening procedure).

The other way of using tests together is sometimes called the composite score method. This involves the use of complex statistical techniques — multiple correlation and regression analysis — that are beyond the scope of the present discussion; see Lewis (1985) for a fuller description. In effect, this method takes the individual correlations established between each test and the criterion, and between the tests themselves. It finds what is the best combination of test information for predicting performance and other criteria and yields a set of weights that can be used in future, which gives the correct emphasis to each piece of test data to maximize the accuracy of the prediction. The composite score approach to combining tests often shows that the power of a battery of a tests is much greater than the individual test validities might indicate. Several separate tests may have correlations with the criterion in the 0.1-0.2 range, but a composite score may produce a correlation of 0.4 or more.

The above discussion assumes that an organization has some data on the relationship between test scores and whatever it is they are trying to predict. Often, that is not the case, so there is no opportunity to find out what the optimum weighting for each test should be. This should not deter them from using a battery of tests and combining their results together on a more intuitive basis to build up a picture of the candidate. Evidence shows that while this is not as effective a way of using the information to predict future performance as is statistical analysis, it can still produce impressive results (Bentz, 1985; Moses, 1985). The range of abilities and qualities that generally need to be considered is in itself a convincing reason for the use of a battery of tests, providing that the battery does not become so large that it is more a test of endurance than of anything else.

Integrating test results with other parts of a selection procedure

When the main stage of the assessment is reached, a number of questions arise. First, if tests have yet to be given, should they be given before or after an interview? The answer is that they are best administered before any interview, so that the results can act as a source of hypotheses that interviewers can probe and test in the interview. Any marked traits or deficiencies might be singled out in this way, especially in relation to personality characteristics. Also any discrepancy between the level of intellectual potential (as shown by the tests) and the individual's level of achievement should be the source of close scrutiny. There is a counter argument that maintains the test results should not be available before the interview so that the interviewers are not biased in their judgements by the information. There is some force in this but overall the balance is definitely in favour of using the results to guide the interview — there are apt to be a lot of queries hanging in the air afterwards if they are not.

Another issue is how much weight to give to the test scores compared to other sources of assessment data, such as academic record, references, interviewers' ratings and so on, and in practice some users place too much weight on test scores and others too little. The evidence on the validity of tests compared with the validity of interview and other information is such as to make a strong case for putting the greatest weight on the psychometric test results (McCormick and Ilgen, 1985). The interview, as it is normally carried out and on its own, has repeatedly been shown to lack both reliability and validity. Much the same can be said of the value of references. Although some studies of references have shown good validity (eg university references about graduates sent to the Civil Service Commission) this cannot be assumed. Academic record and other background facts about the person can contribute significantly to accurate prediction when treated statistically and put together in the form of a 'biodata' question-naire — though this is just mechanistic prediction and does not say anything about the individual as such. By themselves, facts about academic achievements have proved very variable predictors and generalizations are particularly difficult to make. In part this is due to the fact that differences in grades can reflect small differences in marks, that there are different pass rates in different subjects, that there are different Examination Boards and syllabi, and so on. Psychometric tests commonly predict future performance better than do academic results.

The wisest strategy is to gather assessment information from a number of sources rather than to rely completely on any one. None, including psychological tests, is perfect or anywhere near it. Where discrepancies in the findings from these sources arise, they need to be investigated thoroughly. In general, though, the test data are likely to prove the more objective and predictive.

From all that has been said so far on the subject of using tests in decision making, it should be apparent that there are considerable dangers in trying to interpret results in an entirely mechanistic fashion. But this is precisely what some assessment reports generated on microcomputers do; the test or questionnaire data is fed in and the machine produces a series of statements that appear to be justified by the individual scores rather than groups of factors or the total profile. This issue is discussed in more detail in chapter 10.

Access to test results

The increasing use of psychological tests brings with it the danger of the abuse of the information they provide.

Controlling the access to that information is one way of reducing the danger. Ideally, test results should only be available to the individual assessed (in the course of a properly conducted feedback session, of which more anon), to a personnel manager trained in their use, and beyond that on a limited 'need to know' basis. Assuming that the personnel department is arranging the assessment, any access to the results given to line managers — who are likely to be untrained in testing — should be carefully monitored and guided by the personnel managers concerned. Failure to do this is likely to lead to a fair range of horrors, from excessive reliance on the findings (and probably wrongly inter- preted for good measure) to complete disregard of them. There should certainly be no question of copies of test results or the reports written on the basis of them being held anywhere other than in the personnel department and access should be restricted to accredited users. Completed answer sheets and profiles are confidential documents and must be treated as such.

How long should the results of tests be kept and referred to? A rule of thumb on this would be to say the test data has a 'shelf life' of five years and no more than that. People and circumstances change, and to dig out test results from 15 years ago when making a decision about an individual — which has been known to happen — is neither fair nor sensible. Personality data will be more prone to variation over time than will ability scores, though over a very long period there may well be a tendency for verbal ability to improve while other ability scores decrease somewhat. There will be big individual differences in the extent of change over time, some people showing marked changes and some virtually none. The only safe option is to stop using the data after five years and, if the need arises, administer a fresh set of tests. However, data more than five years old should be kept as a source of information about the worth of long-term procedures, such as identification of potential top managers among graduate entrants.

If tests are being used as a sole basis of sifting, a five year gap would seem to be far too long and a much shorter interval would seem appropriate. For example, the Post Office allows existing employees seeking promotion to attempt tests twice within a two year period so that applicants do not feel that too much depends on their performance on a single occasion.

Giving feedback on test results

Throughout this book there has been a great deal of emphasis on the reactions of the person taking the test and on the need to make the experience as acceptable and as stress-free as possible. This is particularly important when internal applicants are being assessed, since good feedback can help to sustain the motivation of those who have been unsuccessful. However, there is growing recognition that feedback to external candidates should help to make the procedure more attractive to them. Further, one of the surest ways of gaining honesty in answering questionnaires is for the candidate to know that there will be some feedback.

Ideally, feedback should be given by someone trained both in testing and in counselling — it requires counselling skill to present results that are not always very positive in such a manner that the individual concerned is both accurately informed of them and still able to maintain motivation and self esteem; see Fletcher (1985, 1986) for further discussion of this.

If at all possible, the feedback should be treated as a confidential discussion so that it does not become an extension of the assessment process in the eyes of the candidate. A fairly common approach to sessions of this kind is to start by seeking the candidate's views and feelings about the tests, then to go through them one by one — always checking that the tests being talked about at each stage are recalled by the individual and that he or she is given the opportunity to comment on the results.

When the basic test data have been conveyed, the discussion moves on to interpreting them in terms of their implications for the individual's behaviour and relationships at work, development needs, career progression and aspirations, and so on. The more the candidate can be encouraged to participate in this interpretation and discussion, the better it is likely to be. It will be in the organization's interests as well that employees or potential employees who have undergone psychometric assessment should be able to use the information obtained in seeking to improve future performance.

It is sometimes possible to give feedback on some aspects of performance (eg test and questionnaire results) during an assessment or immediately afterwards, and this can increase motivation to attend. But there is a strong case for delaying most of the feedback until the outcome of the assessment is known, particularly for internal applicants. The feedback will be much more meaningful if related to the new job or to the prospects for those who have not been successful.

Other options

In chapter 5 there was information about the large-scale testing programmes carried out by major employers such as the Post Office and Civil Service. The question arises as to whether and in what ways feedback can be given to external candidates, particularly when very large numbers of applicants are involved and a very large amount of time might be required.

In part the strategy of the testing organization regarding feedback will depend on the type of test used. If, for example, applicants have attempted a test designed to measure computer programming aptitude which has been used as a first sift, a letter telling applicants that they had not reached a sufficiently high standard to move on to the next stage of the procedure might at first seem adequate. However, it would be helpful to candidates to know whether their rejection was because there were too many candidates with higher scores or whether they simply did not meet the minimum standards; from the point of view of the candidate this could make the difference between trying for programming work elsewhere and making applications for a different kind of work.

Some candidates like to ask questions of someone trained in testing and counselling skills in order to obtain any additional information (eg was the failure 'borderline'? Is the aptitude test widely used?).

While contact by letter or telephone might suffice if a particular skill is being tested, complications may arise if either a range of qualities are being tested or if the candidate has taken part in a more complex procedure such as an assessment centre.

If a range of qualities has been tested, there is more likelihood of the applicant being 'hurt' by the knowledge that he or she has failed to reach the required standard. It is one thing for a person to learn that he/she has not got the aptitude for a particular job, quite another for the person to receive information which suggests he/she has little potential for any job! However, simply to avoid giving feedback does not help the candidate who could benefit by learning about areas of relative strength and being reminded that there are many jobs for which the particular tests used would not be relevant. Again the telephone number of a good trained contact person might be given; an alternative would be for some insight into the results to be passed indirectly to the candidates via trained counsellors and careers advisors with a background in testing. A third possibility is to prepare an appropriate report for the individual using a computer-based 'expert system' (see chapter 10).

If the candidate has attended an assessment centre, the potential problems in giving feedback would seem to be even greater because of the very detailed information that has been collected.

However, the demand for feedback from the candidates is also likely to be high because of the time and, in some cases, personal information they have given. Feedback using the kinds of strategies described above might again be helpful.

A form of feedback that can do more harm than good is simply to send a written copy of the test results or of a report on them to the individual without any amplification. Apart from the fact that things can look a little stark in print, the person concerned is almost certainly untrained in testing and knows next to nothing about what the scores really mean or how the interpretations are arrived at. The scope for misunderstanding is formidable, and there is a good chance that the recipient will be upset by some of what is said. With no opportunity to seek elucidation or to explore the implications of the results with someone who is properly trained, the individual may be worse off than if no feedback had been given at all.

A totally different argument against giving feedback is that it might give candidates more opportunity to question the decisions that have been made. However, if the procedures have been professionaly designed and run by trained staff they should have no difficulty in justifying their point of view.

Summary

Although tests are often used as a means of sifting applicants to decide who will attend the final and more time-consuming parts of the selection procedure, considerable attention may need to be paid to establishing the cut-offs and there is no single best way of doing this; indeed there are a number of pitfalls to be avoided and the actual method chosen will depend on very particular circumstances.

There are also potential pitfalls when using profiles from personality questionnaires; in particular, profiles from occupational groups are often based on all those doing a particular job, and not just those who are successful at it.

Ways of combining test results to increase their predictive power have been outlined, and ways of integrating test results with other parts of the selection procedure have been suggested. On the balance of things, it is recommended that interviewers should know the test scores of applicants before they interview so that the reasons for any apparent discrepancies can be probed.

Finally, the control of access to test scores is strongly recommended. It is also recommended that scores should not be stored for longer than five years unless follow-up studies are planned. The importance of giving the principle of feedback to applicants, particularly those already working within the organization, is discussed and ways of doing this are described.

9
Evaluating a testing programme

This chapter draws together some of the issues raised elsewhere in the book and considers them in more detail:

- How can the worth of a test be assessed, ie is it valid?
- Does the test discriminate fairly?
- Has the testing been worthwhile financially? (Benefits, costs and potential problems).

Once again, the main focus of comments will be on the process of selection.

Checking the worth of a test

Validity is perhaps the most important factor to take into account when evaluating a test, for if the test does not measure what it claims to measure the procedure is pointless.

In an ideal world, the validity of the test or tests chosen would already have been established during a number of similar applications, and the potential confirmed by trials in which the tests were administered at the time of selection but no account taken of results; following such preliminaries it would be possible to predict validity with some confidence. However, the ideal is rarely achieved. For example, consider how an aptitude test for computer programmers might be chosen. First, the work being done by the particular group of programmers would need to be studied; programmers work on different kinds of problems using different computer languages (software) and different computer equipment (hardware). Then, the information available about aptitude tests for computer programmers would need to be considered. If a test were to be a predictor of the performance of just one group of programmers (working on one type of problem using a single language and with one manufacturer's equipment designed three years ago) with what confidence can validity be assumed for other applications?

Other issues can also affect test validity, including the age, educational standard and test sophistication of the applicants. Accordingly it is recommended that studies of the validity of the tests should always be carried out even if evidence of validity elsewhere is strong. The studies can be of three kinds.

Predictive validity is regarded as the best single measure of the worth of a test (see chapter 2). However, there are very few people who have the technical expertise to carry out a proper study of predictive validity and there are a number of methodological and statistical pitfalls which can give misleading results to those who lack professional qualifications and expertise.

However, there are three reasons why those using tests should have some understanding of some of the steps involved in assessing validity. The first is that an understanding of some of the principles will help with the initial choice of tests and/or with the choice of expert advisers. The second is that it can be helpful for personnel managers and others to appreciate the kind of information that will need to be recorded and collated if validation studies are to be carried out. Third, it is important that personnel and other managers know how the worth of tests can be monitored so that they can seek expert advice if there are signs that all is not well.

Local studies which can be of some value are of two kinds:

(i)   subjective evaluation

(ii)   studies involving summarizing data.

Advice on statistical analysis is also given.

(i) Subjective evaluation
An initial form of validation that needs no statistical analysis but which nevertheless has some worth is to consider how the test results match up to observations. If an employee is tested, do the findings 'make sense' in terms of the experience of the person

concerned? While the tests may point up some features or ideas about the individual that are new (if they did not, it would seem to have been fruitless asking for the tests to be done, unless for reassurance), the picture that emerges should not be unrecognizable. However, in view of the 'Barnum' effect (chapter 4) this is best regarded as an interim measure pending the collection of sufficient data for a proper validation study.

When evaluating test results by looking at the way a person behaves once they have been taken on, a danger to guard against is the self-fulfilling prophecy; in other words, people may see only what they expect to see. If the numbers to be followed-up are very small this may be the only kind of analysis that is feasible, but more rigorous approaches should be used if possible.

(ii) Studies which involve summarizing data
Data that can be collected is essentially of three kinds:

- biographical data
- data about test scores
- data about job performance

Biographical data needs to be collected because one of the most important principles of summarizing data is to compare 'like with like'. Test scores may depend on characteristics of those doing the tests (such as their age, sex, ethnic origins) while their job performance may depend on their length of service, education and many other factors other than test scores.

If numbers are small (less than 100) there is a danger that the sample may not be representative and hence any trends must be viewed with caution. Sometimes numbers can be increased by 'pooling' data — for example, by combining the test scores of applicants at different sites or over several years, but it is best to take expert advice if 'pooling' is necessary.

If numbers are sufficient look to see whether there appears to be a marked difference between, for example, the test scores of women under 20 and men over 45. If there are marked differences, keep the groups separate when doing further analysis (see below).

Data about test scores needs to be collected to look at both the number of scores and their range. In order to check the worth of the test it is desirable that the actual test scores cover the full range of possible test scores and that, when drawn on a graph, the pattern of scores approximates to a bell-shaped curve called the normal curve (figure 2). If selection decisions have taken the test scores into account there may be few, if any, low test scores among those taken on and for this reason the curve may not be bell-shaped. To determine whether or not there is a full range and distribution of test scores look at the shape of the curve; also compare the scores of those recruited and those rejected and, in addition, the patterns of these scores compared with those for other groups reported in the test manual.

Figure 2

An illustration of the 'normal curve' using hypothetical test scores; each dots represents an individual obtaining the score.

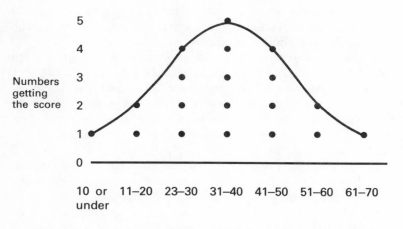

Test scores

Next, data about job performance needs to be collected; the following are possibilities:

Ratings from managers/supervisors

Time to first promotion

Number of promotions gained

Salary growth

Tenure (length of stay)

Absences

Successful completion of training

Sales achieved by the individual

Ideally, several of these measures should be used — otherwise there is a danger of the tests being selected on the basis of their ability to solve one problem (eg reducing the number of low performers being taken on) but at the expense of another (eg a rise in labour turnover).

As with test scores, it is important to look at the distribution of the data that has been collected. For example, it may be found that all those recruited are judged to be at least satisfactory and that few, if any, are judged less than satisfactory or unsatisfactory.

The final stage is to plot onto a series of graphs information combining test scores and job performance; if possible, each graph should comprise similar groups of people (eg females under 21) which are often referred to as sub-groups. These sub-groups can then be combined to form larger groups (eg all females).

Having drawn a series of graphs (or, if the numbers are small, just a single graph) the pattern of scores should be appraised; if the scores approximate to a line (straight, curved or even 'bow shaped') then use can be made of this pattern to predict job performance and the test is almost certainly valid.

If there is no pattern to the test scores, look back at the range of distributions of both the test scores and the measures of job performance. If the scores or measures do not cover a full range, the results may be inconclusive because, for example, it cannot be predicted how people with low scores would have worked out if they had been recruited. Expert advice could then be sought on the application of statistical corrections.

If there is no pattern to the scores *and* there is a full range of test scores and measures of job performance there *may* be problems and it would be wise to seek advice from an occupational psychologist and/or the test suppliers or publishers. However, remember that testing need only be a little bit better than chance to be commercially worthwhile and that marginal trends can be difficult to see visually. Also remember the rest of the selection process such as the interviews may not have been subject to the same scrutiny — do not assume that they would have been better if they were!

(iii) Statistical analyses
The summaries of data described in the previous section can go a long way to establishing whether a test is working. However, questions do arise which cannot be answered by summaries and graphs alone. For example:

- if part of the range of test scores is missing, can the 'true' validity of the test be estimated? (it can!);

- which of two tests with similar graphical results is 'the best'?

- how can scores on different tests be combined together to give the most useful prediction?

- how do test scores compare with predictions from other ratings such as the assessments of interviewers?

Those with some statistical background will find guidance in books (eg Lewis, 1985; The Society for Industrial and Organizational Psychology, 1987) but as in other areas a little knowledge can be a dangerous thing, for example:

- managers in one organization compared test scores for apprentices with subsequent performance and, as a result, wrote an article claiming that tests supplied for apprentice selection were 'useless'; in fact, only those scoring in the top five per cent of marks had been recruited but the lack of range of test scores had not been taken into account when validity had been assessed;

- a manager in another organization suggested changing the design of a test on the basis of two samples of test scores each less than 30 in number; both samples came from the same office; the organization was using 5,000 copies of the test annually spread over a number of locations!

Many different kinds of statistical analysis can be carried out on data from tests and assessments of performance. One common analysis is to determine whether or not the results are statistically significant. A statistically significant result is one that is unlikely to have occurred by chance, and there is a convention of using asterisks to indicate the level of confidence that can be placed in the results. The convention can be summarized thus:

*   means that the probability of result occurring by chance is less than five per cent (using statistical convention p ‹0.05);

**   means the probability of a chance result is less than one per cent (p ‹0.01);

***   means the probability of a chance result is less than 0.1 per cent (p ‹0.001).

When looking at the results of statistical analyses many factors must be taken into account, including the appropriateness of the statistics used. In particular, note that:

- small sample sizes make it less likely that statistically significant results will be found;

- correlations may be of little practical value even if they are statistically significant; for example, correlations less than 0.10 would not normally be regarded as worthwhile for selection predictions;

- correlations do not imply causation or explanations; for example, there *might* be a correlation between cups of tea drunk each day and take home pay but people cannot increase their take home pay by drinking more tea.

Accordingly, it is recommended that expert advice is taken from occupational psychologists who specialize in test validation (see appendix 1). Their access to computing facilities will often speed the calculations that need to be made.

Does the test discriminate fairly?

Effective tests discriminate on the basis of job-relevant characteristics. However, unfair discrimination should be avoided for a number of reasons. For example, it can be challenged on commercial grounds − if an organization is precluding large numbers of potential applicants because of their sex, ethnic origin, etc, it may have difficulty in filling vacancies and surviving in the future. This would be critical for any British companies seeking American Government contracts since such contracts are dependent on effective equal opportunities policies. In addition, it is important that any organization aiming to provide a service to a wide cross section of the community should be sensitive to a range of needs. Unfair discrimination can also be challenged because it is illegal and because suspicion of unfair discrimination can lead to costly enquiries; for example, industrial tribunals can be costly both in terms of meeting damages or other awards and in terms of the time the staff may need to prepare for the tribunal and to attend it. Further, there can be adverse public relations implications affecting both the perceived worth of top management and the attractiveness of the organization to potential employees.

Checks should be made to ensure that tests are not discriminating unfairly against:

- members of one sex
- members of ethnic minority groups
- disabled people
- applicants of different ages.

Two kinds of check need to be made. The first is to see whether there are differences between sub-groups in terms of the range and distribution of the test scores. By way of example, assume that two clerical tests (A and B) are being tried out; the form of the trial is to administer both tests to all applicants but not to take the scores into account when making selection decisions.

At the end of the trial period a simple first analysis would involve computing summary tables of test scores for each test for each sub-group of interest; in table 4, 50 male and 50 female candidates are being compared; both tests have a score range from 0 to 50. The distribution of scores achieved on Test A is the same for both men and women and at this stage the test does not discriminate unfairly against members of either sex. In contrast, women have done much better on Test B and, if a single cut-off point were to be used when selecting staff, unfair discrimination could be a problem; for example, if the cut-off point were to be 21, 23 men would be recruited and 37 women.

Table 4

| | Numbers achieving these scores | | | |
| | Test A | | Test B | |
Test Score	Male	Female	Male	Female
41–50	10	10	5	15
31–40	10	10	8	12
21–30	10	10	10	10
11–20	10	10	12	8
0–10	10	10	15	5

(NB   The range of scores achieved on a test will usually approximate to the normal curve shown in figure 2 — tables 4 and 5 have been simplified for the purposes of illustration).

There has been speculation about whether a second kind of discrimination might arise because the effectiveness of a test might vary from group to group, and this possibility should be checked too. The possibility is illustrated in the following example involving Test A only. Imagine that six months after giving the test to the last of the applicants in the trial, the performance of the applicants is assessed and the relationship between test scores and job performance is tabulated; the results are shown in table 5.

Table 5
Job performance

scores on test	Male and female combined		Male		Female	
	acceptable	unacceptable	acceptable	unacceptable	acceptable	unacceptable
A						
41-50	16	4	7	3	9	1
31-40	14	6	6	4	8	2
21-30	12	8	5	5	7	3
11-20	10	10	4	6	6	4
0-10	8	12	4	6	4	6

For Test A, table 4 had shown no obvious unfair discrimination in the scores achieved by each sex. However, table 5 shows a different predictive relationship between test score and job performance for men and women: a score of 11 or above indicates 60 per cent probability of acceptable job performance for women, while men need to achieve a score of 31 for the probability of acceptable job performance to be at the same level.

Thus while an overall pass mark of 21 would give a 60 per cent probability of acceptable job performance, this could be viewed as a discrimination against women whose chances of success would be 60 per cent with only a score of 11.

Thus, if a single cut-off is used, tests may discriminate unfairly against a particular sub-group because of differences in the overall distribution of test scores achieved and/or because of differences in the predictive relationship between test and job performance.

If findings of this kind arise in either case, the following issues need to be considered:

(i)   first, have the numbers involved in analysis been large enough for statistically reliable conclusions to be drawn? Table 7 is based on 100 people but when divided into 20 'cells' some of the numbers are small and none are above double figures; this is one reason why total groups of 200 or more are desirable for statistical purposes;

(ii) second, could other factors be at play? eg, in the case of clerical tests, male applicants may not have studied relevant subjects at school;

(iii) third, consider taking other action.

Each of these points will now be considered in turn.

(i)   Sample sizes

In order to draw accurate conclusions about the occurrence of unfair discrimination, there should ideally be at least 100 people in each of the sub-groups that are of interest. However, any gross differences may be apparent from samples half that size. While test users can often obtain adequate samples of male and female applicants, they can find it difficult to obtain sufficient numbers from different ethnic minority groups. (This raises the separate issue of how to categorize and group such individuals for this type of analysis — a complex issue in itself.)

If numbers are very small, they can sometimes be built up by reference to data collected about previous intakes of staff, to data collected about the same test by other employers, or to data collected by the test publisher. If a new and unproven test shows signs of unfair discrimination, results should not be taken into account at the time of selection and the validity of the test and the reasons for discrimination expertly investigated as soon as a sufficient sample has built up.

(ii) Circumstances
If differences in test performance are based on substantial sample sizes the underlying reasons should be investigated. It may be found, for example, that if previous experience (or lack of it) seems to be the reason for differences in performance some of the effects of previous experience might be overcome by offering relevant experience prior to testing (eg a special short course).

(iii) Taking other action
The following possibilities should be considered and expert advice taken on them:

- Can an alternative test be found which is equally effective in terms of predictive validity but which does not discriminate?

- Can the test be redesigned so that those items which are discriminating unfairly are dropped?

- Can alternative tests (or even alternative methods of selection) be offered to applicants? For example, potential applicants could be sifted by either passing public or internal examinations, or by passing an aptitude test, or by passing a job-related training course.

If none of the above possibilities are feasible, the apparent conflict between the spirit and the letter of the law presents real problems for responsible employers wishing to comply with currrent legislation. The dilemma is illustrated by the following example. Suppose that for several years tests have been administered to

2,000 applicants (1,000 male and 1,000 female) in order to shortlist 100 for interview, and that the same pass mark has been used for both groups. Follow-up shows that this has resulted in 70 males being called for interview and 30 females, ie seven per cent of males and three per cent of females. Follow-up also shows that the test has been an effective predictor of performance, so there is reluctance to consider any of the alternatives described above.

Under these circumstances an employer wishing to observe the spirit of the law might continue to shortlist the seven per cent of males but to increase the number of females shortlisted to seven per cent as well. This would increase the numbers that are shortlisted but would avoid the challenge that males are being disadvantaged (seven per cent would still be called for shortlisting) or that females were the subject of discrimination (the percentage called forward would now be identical to that for the men).

While such a strategy might satisfy the spirit of the law its operation in the example given would depend on the use of lower 'pass' marks for women. This would appear to conflict with the current legislation which requires that all candidates taking the same procedure are treated equally.

Where such conflicts are apparent in legislation it is normal for them to be resolved by either the hearing of a test case so that law can be established or by revision of the legislation.

The same principles can be followed when scrutinizing for fairness among ethnic minority groups and disabled people. Remember that in order to be able to check the fairness of the tests (and the whole selection procedure) in this way, appropriate details must be collected from applicants at the time of selection.

Scrutiny for fairness should not be confined to tests. In particular, make sure that interviewers have received appropriate training and monitor their assessments with the same rigour as for test scores; Professor Robert Guion has drawn attention to the need to check the fairness not only of the selection methods but also the decision making process and the individual decision makers.

Readers who wish to go into this very complex area are recommended to obtain a booklet entitled *Discriminating Fairly: A Guide to Fair Selection* which was published jointly by the British Psychological Society and the Runnymede Trust, or one of the other specialist publications in this area (eg Pearn 1979).

Benefits, costs and potential problems

The benefits, costs and potential problems are considered under the following headings:

(i)   the potential benefits of testing to the employing organization;

(ii)   the costs of testing to the employing organization;

(iii) other risks and possible costs.

(i)   Potential benefits of testing to the employing organization

The essential benefits of testing to the employing organization can be considered under two broad headings: financial benefits and other benefits.

Financial benefits

The use of tests can lead to substantial financial benefit for two reasons:

(a)   the quality of selection and hence the productivity of employees may be improved; further there may be other benefits such as improved quality of work, reduced turnover etc;

(b)   the cost of processing large numbers of applications can be minimized.

(a)   Improving the quality of selection: Tests can provide measurements of qualities which it may be difficult or impossible to assess at selection by any other means. Examples range from aptitude for computer programming to dexterity for particular tasks. The correct use of tests can therefore allow the organization to make a better match beween an individual and a job. The use of tests can thus contribute to the cost effectiveness of selection in three ways. First, because the job performance of those taken on may prove to be better than if tests were not used. Second, because those selected by the improved methods may need less training and stay longer, thus reducing an organization's recruitment and training bills. Third, because those taken on may be more suitable than external applicants when it comes to promotion

to a higher level and hence the cost of subsequent recruitment may also be reduced. However, the needs of subsequent jobs will have to be taken into account at the time of selection if this third benefit is to be achieved.

In a job where performance can be measured objectively, it is possible to calculate the actual financial savings which can be achieved by improving selection and thus increasing output or reducing the numbers of employees required to meet the output targets. (Schmidt and Hunter, 1979; Hunter and Schmidt, 1982; Smith, 1986). In a recent paper describing assessment centres (including psychometric tests) used in the selection of senior police and prison officers, Bedford and Feltham (1986) estimated annual net savings of over 1.3 million pounds.

For many management jobs it is not possible to quantify the actual savings in this way, but the financial benefit to be gained by an organization from making a good selection decision is potentially far greater. In many cases it may not only be the salary and overheads associated with employing the individual which are at stake, but the future prospects of the company if a bad decision is made.

(b) Minimizing the cost of processing large numbers of applications: Mention has already been made of the use of tests as a way of 'sifting' applications; the aim of sifting is to increase the final selection ratio (see chapter 5).

Other potential benefits of testing

Monitoring and maintenance of standards: The use of tests allows comparison between applicants both over time and at different places. Tests can therefore help in the maintenance of selection standards from year to year among areas and regions both within and outside an organization. Most commercially available tests have a wide range of norms available which allow comparisons to be made with similar applications to other organizations, although such data is normally supplied in confidence by the users to the test publishers and the names of the supplying organizations may not be known to other users. Large organizations may have enough data to draw up their own comparative norms as well. The standard of individual applicants can be compared and one applicant group can be judged against another. Without tests, it is more difficult to make objective comparisons and it is likely to be some time before variation in the standard of applicants, and thus possibly recruits, become evident — possibly to the cost of the employing organization.

Attracting better applicants: Some organizations believe that the use of tests helps to attract better applicants. This was certainly the case when War Office Selection Boards for officer selection replaced recommendations made by commanding officers after 15 minute interviews. Under the system of recommendations, stories had got around that it was no good putting up for a commission unless you had won your colours at cricket and rode to hounds (Toplis and Stewart, 1983). More recently, graduate applicants indicated that they chose a particular organization because they were impressed by the opportunities they were given to show the skills and abilities they had. (They often have little else to go on.) The more systematic and professional the selection procedure, the more likely it is to be perceived by the candidate as fair and effective. (Rynes *et al*, 1980).

Encouraging self-selection: Some tests convey information to the candidate about the nature and content of the job for which they have applied thus encouraging self-selection and increasing the likelihood of the organization getting the best person for the job.

Improving candidates' self perception: The very process of taking tests may help candidates to improve their self perception and thus contribute to their being able to make a better choice of career and organization, whether or not they are offered or take the particular job for which they have applied. If tests are used widely, this could provide a broader benefit to all organizations by leading to a better match between individuals and jobs.

(ii) Costs of testing to the employing organization
Against the anticipated financial and other benefits, the potential user must set the cost of gaining access to testing expertise and introducing and sustaining a testing programme. Here the main issues in terms of costs are summarized.

Gaining access to testing expertise
Ways of gaining access to testing expertise, and the costs involved, were described in chapter 4.

Introducing and sustaining a testing programme
Once testing expertise is available there are four main stages in introducing and sustaining a testing programme; first, training test administrators, second, obtaining the materials, third, monitoring the programme and fourth, reviewing the programme. The costs likely to be incurred at each of these stages are as follows:

(a) *Training accredited testers.* Training often involves residential training courses. Costs are incurred both for the registration and residential fees, and also as a result of absence from work. In 1987, the cost of one week's residential training was up to 1,000 pounds excluding VAT. Because courses differ in the tests offered, training venues etc, there can be marked differences in fees charged.

(b) *Obtaining test materials.* Such a range and diversity of psychological tests are available that it is impossible to give any idea of typical costs in this book. However, in 1987 some question booklets cost up to 5 pounds and some answer sheets up to 1 pound. Catalogues and price lists are produced annually by most suppliers; current price lists should be checked by organizations who are calculating the costs of introducing testing. At least one publisher also charges licencing fees which, in 1987, were up to 1,000 pounds per test. Although costs can be substantial, these are minor compared with the costs incurred if, for example, errors are made in the appointment of senior managers whose influence may extend well beyond their own department.

(c) *Monitoring a testing programme.* Once a testing system is established, organizations need to allocate resources for monitoring tests to make sure they are being used properly; without such monitoring it is possible that some of those administering tests may fall into bad habits — it is surprising how many test administrators are tempted to alter the time allowed for tests, etc. 'Monitoring' can also involve making sure that managers do not start to develop their own tests — some are tempted to do so because they do not realize the ways in which a test should be developed, constructed and normed, nor do they appreciate the rigours of administration and scoring, the use of norms for assessment, the possibility of unfair discrimination and so on.

(d) *Reviewing a testing programme.* Jobs often evolve over time and the relationship between a particular test and job performance may therefore have changed. Educational and employment opportunities may also affect the numbers and quality of applicants coming forward. Accordingly, the validity of every test should be checked ar regular intervals (eg every five years, and more frequently if there are distinct changes in all or any of these areas).

(iii) Other risks and possible costs

The main areas where costs will be incurred have now been described. However, there are also other, non-financial, risks accompanying testing which an organization should be aware of and consider. These are obtaining effective tests, test security, test popularity, possible adverse effects on candidates, possible outside scrutiny, registration under the Data Protection Act.

Obtaining effective tests

Selecting the right test for the right situation is not always easy. Ghiselli (1966) examined the results of many studies which had been conducted on the validity of tests in the selection and placement of workers in a wide range of occupations and found large variations in validity. Several ideas have been put forward as to why such variations may be occurring, including the possibility of inappropriate tests being used.

Another possible pitfall is the unsuccessful transfer of the use of a test or tests which have been successful in selecting applicants in one situation. Even jobs with identical titles may have differences which affect the ability of the test to predict job success and the differences may not be apparent if only superficial enquiries are made. For example, there may be differences in the level of responsibility and decisions to be made, in the type of figure work to be done, in the equipment to be used, in the way the work is supervised, in the noise, heating or other environmental conditions and so on.

Test security

From time to time there are reports of tests being compromised. For example, one company found its manual dexterity test — involving placing washers and nuts onto screw threads — had been studiously copied and that some applicants were attending for practice at a nearby house before going on to the company for their proper test. While there is nothing wrong with practice sessions *per se*, and indeed many tests have a built-in supervised practice session, it is important in selection to treat all applicants equally; either all applicants should have opportunities to practice for the specified and carefully timed period or no-one should.

Accordingly, every effort *must* be made to maintain test security (eg applicants should not have the opportunity to copy the test materials) and if tests are heavily used parallel forms should be professionally developed so that applicants are unlikely to know the particular version that they are given.

Test popularity

The popularity of some commercially available tests can lead to further difficulties. For example, in graduate recruitment it is possible that the same applicant will take the same tests in several different organizations within a relatively short period of time since there are relatively few different tests available for graduate recruitment in the UK. In general this is likely to result in some applicants steadily improving their scores as they remember some 'correct' answers and thus have more time to work out answers to other questions, but exceptions have been noted. It is important to establish whether or not previous experience of the tests is affecting results — if test scores are enhanced by prior experience, unsuitable candidates may be 'passed', while if prior experience depresses scores, suitable candidates may be rejected.

It is also important to consider the possibility that some applicants might have distorted their responses to psychometric questionnaires in an attempt to 'improve' the profile that they obtained on a previous occasion.

Possible adverse effects on candidates

A potential problem in the use of tests is that some applicants may lack confidence in their own abilities and not put themselves forward if testing is involved. The possibility of intimidation is a particular problem when dealing with less academic school leavers, disabled candidates, older candidates, people trying to return to work after a period of non-employment, etc. However, in order to try and overcome this problem and minimize any advantage or disadvantage to particular groups which could arise from their 'ability to take tests', many tests have example questions for candidates to do in their own time, before starting the proper test; the example questions enable the candidates to familiarize themselves with the formats of the questions and reduce their fears. Another way to deal with this is to provide applicants with a handout explaining, in friendly non-technical language, why tests are being used and giving example questions (see chapter 7). The use of computers and/or recorded instructions may also help to minimize any fears (see chapter 10).

Possible outside scrutiny

Organizations who use tests may have to justify their actions to bodies such as the Equal Opportunities Commission (EOC) or the the Commission for Racial Equality (CRE) and appropriate analyses were described earlier in this chapter. The EOC and CRE may wish to look into the origins and worth of a test if a complaint about its fairness is made. However, there is no reason to think that either the EOC or CRE will look at a test any more than they look at any other aspect of selection procedures, including application forms and interviews. If the content of the test has been carefully matched to the requirements of the job and its use is based on past experience of the reasons for success and failure (as it should be), it is very unlikely that either body will find any reason to investigate. Nevertheless, care should be taken that tests avoid the use of colloquial English, and do not assume knowledge more likely to be known by one sex than the other, one racial group than another etc.

Registration under the Data Protection Act

If test scores linked to the individuals' names are to be kept on computer, it is necessary that the employing organization registers this under the terms of the Data Protection Act. If an organization's computer system is already registered under the Act, it should be only an administrative formality to add an extra item (ie test scores) to the specification. However, once individuals are granted rights of access to personal details which are held on computer, organizations whose systems include test scores will have to develop procedures for providing individuals with meaningful feedback about their performance and take appropriate steps regarding copyright (see chapter 5); raw scores alone are at best meaningless and at worst dangerous and open to misinterpretation (see chapters 8 and 10).

Test results should not stay on the computer after their useful life unless they are to form part of a validation or other study (see chapter 8). Also, steps must be taken to ensure that only accredited users have access to this information.

Summary

This chapter has described three possible ways of establishing the worth of tests, and how checks can be made as to whether or not the tests are discriminating fairly.

The benefits, costs and potential problems involved in testing have been drawn together under the following headings:

- the potential benefits
- the main potential costs
- other risks and possible costs.

10
Current developments and keeping informed

At the time of writing there are signs that the future use of tests in the UK will be influenced by the following trends:

- a considerable increase in the use of advanced selection methods;
- the application of small business computer and other electronic equipment;
- Government legislation;
- changes in the way that the British Psychological Society seeks to maintain professional standards in testing.

The chapter ends with guidance as to how to keep abreast of these and other developments.

The increased use of advanced selection methods

On both sides of the Atlantic there has been an increasing use of assessment centre techniques during the last decade, and tests often feature in such procedures. In the UK, an Institute of Personnel Management survey in 1977 found that four per cent of its members were using such methods; a comparable survey in 1985 showed that 21 per cent were now using such methods; within these findings it was noted that 74 per cent of large companies (employing 500+) made use of such methods.

For certain kinds of selection the use of tests has become commonplace as, for example, in the recruitment of graduate entrants. In particular, it has been estimated that 10 per cent of all graduates leaving British universities are employed by accountancy companies, and several of the larger accountancy companies are using increasingly sophisticated selection methods to try and hold or even increase their 'share' of the available applicants. Computer companies and other information technology organizations are also major employers. The scene is further complicated by the fall in the numbers graduating each year because of the fall in the birth rate and because of cut-backs in the universities. Unless the demand for graduates drops, the competition among employers will increase.

Such trends mean that those who employ graduates and other groups of employees where recruitment is difficult (eg computer programmers) are constantly having to re-evaluate their selection methods and employment packages. Those who do not use tests may be under pressure to do so for fear of missing the best talent and/or being left with applicants whom others reject; those who do use tests may be concerned about candidates attempting the tests with other employers (and hence improving their scores a little) and about putting potential candidates off because of the length and difficulty of the selection procedure.

From time to time some employers try different approaches to recruitment, eg by awarding scholarships to undergraduates, by offering vacation work to potential applicants, or by offering specialist training (eg in computer programming) to those without previous experience or relevant degrees. Others have concentrated on ways of attracting applicants, including sending their representatives to universities (the so-called 'milk round') and putting more effort into publicity material, including videos.

Computers and other electronic equipment

Computer technology is influencing testing by providing new methods of administering, scoring, interpreting and monitoring testing. It is also providing new ways of testing and of test development. Each area of innovation is separate but once access to computer equipment is available changes are likely to take place in several areas. Readers should note that the laws of copyright apply and that placing a test or associated information (such as answers or norms) on a computer without the publisher's agreement constitutes infringement of copyright.

Each area of innovation is now discussed in turn, detailing first the potential benefits and then the possible disadvantages.

(i) Test administration

The use of small business and other computers offer many potential advantages (French, 1986) over tests in a pencil and paper form. For example:

- a wider variety of test content can be used (particularly those involving perceptual tasks and response times);

- the facility for 'adaptive' or 'tailored' testing becomes available; adaptive testing means those taking the test can, on the basis of the speed and correctness of response, be moved through the test to those items for which their chances of success are close to 50 per cent; the test is completed when a sample of these items has been attempted and thus the time required for testing can be considerably shortened; in turn this shortened time can help to make the testing procedure more acceptable to the candidates;

- the distribution of test material may be simplified if testing continues to be carried out at several locations. Instead of sending out question booklets, answer sheets etc, it may be sufficient to send out small floppy discs which can then be used over and over again until such time as the test is revised. Because of the small size of the floppy discs the cost of registered postage and other charges are likely to be considerably lower, while the security of the tests is likely to be as high if not higher;

- a high level of standardization can be achieved in the administration of tests by computer; computer-administered tests can be virtually self administering — the role of the administrator can be to check the applicant's name, to sit him or her in front of the keyboard and screen, and to tell the applicant what to do if help is required, or if there is a problem with the equipment, etc. After this very brief person-to-person contact the applicant can be left to read the instructions on the computer screen and comprehension can be checked by appropriate questions; in particular the timing of the tests can be carried out by the computer equipment, avoiding problems due to the lack of a stopwatch or a similarly accurate timer, inaccurate timing arising from human error, and even a wish by the test administrator to alter the times allowed to increase the chances of success. The motives for altering times range from empathy with the candidates (or lack of it) through to the need to fill vacancies, or even the fact that recruiters are sometimes paid bonuses according to the number of staff they take on and therefore want to get as many through the test as possible;

- the use of computers and the range of techniques that they offer for both presenting questions and collecting replies can help in the assessment of handicapped and disabled people;

- a number of studies have been carried out to see whether applicants prefer computer-administered tests to those administered in other ways; unfortunately, some of these studies have been based on an unsatisfactory experimental design, eg one study involved asking people who have taken the computer-administered test whether they preferred it to the pencil and paper version, but without having the pencil and paper version available for inspection. While studies have so far failed to identify any group of applicants for whom the computer-administered test was not the preferred choice, there remains concern that some groups (eg older people) may find the different presentation off-putting;

- once available, computers can help organize the testing programme, eg by producing letters to be sent to candidates, programmes for interviewers, etc.

It is clear that there are many advantages to computer administration. The disadvantages are as follows:

- the lack of personal contact and interest that a test administrator can give may mean that some candidates lose interest;

- the test has to be designed (or redesigned) for computer administration. If a computerized version of a test does not exist, programming expertise will be involved; also it must not be assumed that results from a pencil and paper test and a version of the test which is computer-administered are directly comparable because, for example, there may not be the same opportunity for the candidate to ask questions of the administrators. Even if changes have been kept to a minimum the effect of relatively subtle changes may be important. For example, on a pencil and paper test, candidates may mark questions about which they are uncertain and return to them after they have attempted all the other items; the facility to mark and go back to questions in a computerized version of the test may not be available. Accordingly different norms and cut-offs may have to be developed and used according to whether candidates have taken the pencil and paper or computerized versions of a test;

- the initial finance required for computerized testing can be high, particularly if large groups of candidates need to be tested at the same time and large numbers of computers or terminals are therefore required. In theory it might be possible to offset the cost by using the equipment for other purposes; thus a group of six terminals might be used for training in computing or other subjects when not required for testing; costs may also be kept down by making use of existing terminals or other computer equipment but in practice:

   the equipment may not be free to be used for testing;

   the equipment may not be suitable from a technical point of view (eg the computer language may be inappropriate, the computer memory may be too small, etc);

   the location of the equipment may make it unsuitable for testing, eg a number of terminals may exist but be located on the desks of key staff in a number of busy offices with telephone and other background noises; thus the environment may be totally unsuitable for testing;

   a fourth problem with computerised administration concerns the storage of responses. Under the Data Protection Act, individuals are entitled to a copy of the information stored about them on computer. To protect copyright, they may be denied access to any records of their replies to individual questions, but once the replies have been scored it would seem appropriate to allow access to at least the total scores on tests or sub tests; precisely what applicants can demand will no doubt be established by test cases in the courts of law;

finally, it is possible that the results of adaptive or tailored testing could also be challenged legally because applicants are not being given identical tests; such a challenge is considered unlikely in America because of the familiarity of the judges, prosecutors and defendants with the principle of test design and with the *Standards for Educational and Psychological Testing*, recently published by three eminent American organizations including the American Psychological Association (1985). It remains to be seen whether adaptive testing will be challenged in the UK.

Standard administration can also be achieved through the use of sound and/or video recordings produced to professional standards. Applicants can be given a general welcome and then the recording started. As well as the general instructions and practice, for example, timing can be recorded too. Such an approach has potential when testing is carried out at a number of locations.

(ii) Scoring

Small business and other computers can score tests at high speed; and this is nearly always done if the test is administered on the computer. For tests which are administered in a pencil and paper forms, special answer sheets can be designed; subsequently, by means of a document reader, the replies on the answer sheets can be transferred into a computer. As well as scoring, there is often the facility to show how an individual score relates to a reference group — this is done by means of the percentile scores, the allocation of scores to grades, etc. Some computer bureaux and university and polytechnic departments can offer facilities for document reading and analysis on a consultancy basis.

The main potential disadvantage of computerized scoring concerns its reliability when, in particular, the equipment is used for the first time (see the earlier section on Test Development). In addition, the special equipment for 'reading' replies on printed answer sheets is sufficiently expensive for a high through-put of testing to be necessary for it to pay its way. Accordingly, it may only make financial sense to keep such equipment at a central point rather than have a number of machines at all the places where testing may be carried out.

(iii) Interpretation

Scoring can end with the production of a series of test scores for an individual. For an aptitude test this might include 'raw score' (usually the number of items correct), and the percentile score. For a personality questionnaire, the results might be given in the form of raw scores on a number of personality traits or other dimensions, and a profile might be produced so that the salient personality features for each individual can be seen with relative ease. In both instances the results may then be passed to a psychologist or personnel manager trained in testing who may make a decision on the basis of the results and his or her background knowledge about the tests; alternatively, and perhaps more likely, such assessors may seek to collect further relevant information during later stages of the assessment procedure (eg at interview) before making a decision.

However, the scoring need not end with a numerical summary being provided for human decision making. In some ways it is a relatively small step to print additional words (such as pass and fail) alongside the aptitude test results, basing the printed judgement on a decision-making model supplied by the person running or organizing the testing programme. In fact computers have been used to develop much more elaborate schemes; for example, one long established personality questionnaire has recently become the basis of a computer print-out about suscepti- bility to stress, while other schemes are attempting to give information about jobs and careers that an individual may consider on the basis of aptitude tests and questionnaire replies.

Such schemes have their attractions since the computers can be programmed to take into account systematically large amounts of information both about people and about potential jobs. Thus large numbers of people can be systematically processed and skilled staff need not be involved.

On the other hand, there is much to be questioned. First, there are the normal questions to be asked about the level of confidence that can be placed in the test scores or questionnaire replies. Next there is the level of confidence that can be placed in the descriptions of the available jobs, particularly as individuals can differ in their views about the attractions and disadvantages of the same job. Third, there is the issue of the decision-making model that is being used. Whose model is it? Has the model been agreed by a group of recognized experts, or does it represent the views of a single unqualified individual?

At best computer-generated reports are produced by 'expert systems' which not only consider the score on each scale or dimension but also assess the total picture of personality that is being given in the way that a trained and experienced assessor may look for patterns which support each other, patterns which conflict and so on. But even then some psychologists are of the view that personality questionnaire results are best used as a starting point for possible lines of enquiry and discussion during an interview rather than a firm and permanent picture of personality. Such psychologists would argue that even if a full print-out is available it is best restricted to experienced assessors able to interpret the questionnaire without the computer interpretation; in this way the print-out becomes a possible short cut to an assessment rather than a blind act of faith.

At worst, the computer-generated reports are produced by suspect systems in which individual scores 'trigger' statements mechanistically; because there is no attempt to integrate the overall pattern of replies, important information may be missed and misleading pictures may therefore be given. Accordingly, it is particularly important to seek independent evidence about the validity of a particular system.

(iv) Monitoring
Among activities that need to be carried out, and which are speeded by the use of small business or other computers, are the following:

- the establishment of test norms for the organization/site (so that these can be compared with those for other organizations);

- the establishment of norms for sub groups of applicants (eg by age, sex, ethnic origin) to check that the tests are 'fair';

- the comparison of information about the test scores of individuals and the performance of the same individuals during training and subsequently on the job; (see chapter 9).

(v) Test development
It is clear that small business and other computers can aid aspects of test development. First, they offer the opportunity for different

kinds of test design to be given trial runs. In particular, computers can be programmed to measure both speed and accuracy of response, a facility which is particularly useful if reaction times are to be measured. Second, the collection and storage of test results and other information can speed the statistical analysis which needs to be carried out as a new test is developed. For example, individual items in the test can be ranked in order of difficulty, norms established for the overall group testing and the various sub groups (age, sex, ethnic origin). Third, small business computers offer the facility to change the design of the test at low cost compared with the cost of revising printed test materials.

But while the benefits to be gained may be substantial, the cost implications need to be assessed and monitored carefully. In particular, some types of test involve questions in the form of drawings and the use of graphics can make heavy demands on computer memories; in turn this means that the cost of developing the test may not be viable or that all testing has to be done at a central point to make use of a small number of sophisticated machines. One organization which has developed a high technology system is the Dutch Civil Service which has linked small business computers with video discs instead of storing graphics on computer memories; however, the equipment is expensive and for this reason testing has been centralized.

The time required for test development can sometimes be underestimated because of teething troubles with the new technology — for example, during the development of one test battery the computer failed to 'read' about half the answer sheets and major delays followed. Several products have proved unreliable in user trials.

Government legislation

When setting up or maintaining a programme of testing the following government legislation should be borne in mind:

- the legislation barring discrimination on the grounds of sex or race; in Northern Ireland there is also legislation barring discrimination on religious grounds;

- the legislation encouraging the employment of disabled people;

- the Data Protection Act which concerns the storage of personal information on computers.

(i)   Avoiding unfair discrimination

Compared with other selection methods most tests produce objective and quantifiable results. Accordingly their 'fairness' has attracted legal and other scrutiny on both sides of the Atlantic.

However, test users are unlikely to discriminate unfairly if they follow the steps detailed in this book, viz:

- to base their choice of tests on the requirements of the job to be filled;

- if a choice of tests is available, to select the one which previous studies have shown to be least affected by sex and ethnic origin; information of this kind is unlikely to be available unless the tests have been professionally developed;

- to monitor the effectiveness and fairness of the tests in use; if differences are found which could indicate discrimination, changes could be made to the test items (with the aid of the test designers and publishers). There has from time to time been speculation about a possible alternative approach in which a series of different test norms would be available so that applicants are judged against others with similar characteristics; however, since positive discrimination is illegal in the UK the legal implications of such a strategy may deter some employers from this potential course of action.

Scrutiny should extend beyond tests to other selection methods, to decision making processes and to the fairness and accuracy of individual decision makers (see chapter 9).

(ii)   Recruiting disabled people

It is possible that a disabled candidate will have difficulty in doing an aptitude test but will be perfectly competent at doing the job for which he/she is applying; this could happen, for example, if a pencil and paper version of a test were to be given to a partially sighted person applying for work which did not involve reading or writing. When assessing disabled people avoid aptitude tests which involve skills affected by disability but which are unrelated to the requirements of the job. Instead, consider any special training that the disabled person has received and use trade tests based on samples of real work. Trainability tests may also be helpful. If it is important to look at underlying aptitudes and normal aptitude tests seem inappropriate, specialist advice should be sought.

(iii)   The Data Protection Act

Under the Data Protection Act, companies wishing to store personal information about employees on computers are obliged both to register and to let individuals see the contents of their computer files.

From the point of view of checking the worth of selection procedures it is helpful to store test scores and other information on computers and then to retrieve it for the purposes of validation; this in turn means that individuals are in a position to request to see their test scores.

If the assessment has only been concerned with suitability for a specific job, it is suggested that a handout is prepared which gives brief details of the tests and what the scores mean in terms of decisions about the specific job; it should be stressed that scores only reflect suitability for specific jobs (rather than suitability for *all* jobs); under these circumstances there is little danger of an individual being offended or even hurt by knowledge of the test results (see chapter 8).

However, potential difficulties may arise if test results with wider implications (such as personality questionnaire results) are stored on computer; for reasons described earlier it is preferable that individuals receive feedback about their results at the time of completing the questionnaires and if this is done problems may be avoided; again the preparation of the handout will be preferable to leaving an individual to try to interpret his or her profile; indeed, in view of the time that will be required to enter a profile onto a computer and of potential copyright problems if blank profiles are copied without the permission of the test designers and publishers, it might be best not to put such information on the computer in the first place!

Possible changes in legislation

Governments of different political parties take different views about the need for legislation regarding employment and the extent to which they are prepared to enforce the legislation.

However, it should be emphasized that UK legislation has

tended to endorse professional practice and that if tests are used in accordance with the guidelines in this book both effective selection and the avoidance of unfair discrimination are likely to result.

At the time of writing there are moves in Parliament to extend the principles of the Data Protection Act beyond records kept on computers; in other words, people may be given the right to see all records kept about them, whether on computer or not. This could have major implications for test users — it would certainly be bad practice to allow people access to their personality profiles without interpretation by a qualified person (see chapter 8).

For the future we would speculate that there might eventually be legislation against discrimination on the grounds of age. Ageing brings both advantages and disadvantages in terms of recruitment, and there are at least as many stereotypes and assumptions about older (and younger) people as in other areas of recruitment. Certainly many test scores do vary with age, but the age of maximum performance varies both with the type of test and with experience, training and fitness of the individual applicants. Actual job performance varies with age too!

Keeping informed about future developments

Within the UK, the main source of information about aptitude and other tests comes from psychologists whose professional organization is the British Psychological Society (see address at end of booklet). Leading occupational psychologists belong to the Division of Occupational Psychology, which vets people's experience and competence as practitioners before accepting them as members and from 1988 its members will become Chartered Occupational Psychologists. Readers are strongly advised to employ only psychologists with this qualification whose names and addresses appear in a Register published by the BPS.

The British Psychological Society also publishes the *Guidance and Assessment Review*, a journal devoted to the critical review of assessment and counselling methods, and other articles covering pratical and political issues relating to assessment and counselling. It also contains up to date information on courses in testing to be held during the following two to three months, and reviews of recent academic research of relevance.

The BPS also publishes an academic journal called *Occupational*

Psychology and runs conferences and other events for psychologists; non-psychologists can attend many conferences and other events by invitation; some of these conferences and events cover the use of psychological tests and related methods such as assessment centres.

International organizations may find it helpful to keep in touch with psychological societies, test publishers and leading consultants in the countries in which they are operating. Such information is available from the International Test Commission (see address at end of book) whose objectives are to compare practices in the use of tests throughout the world.

This book has been published under the auspices of the Institute of Personnel Management which has some 30,000 members in the United Kingdom. Articles on the use of tests are published in its monthly publication, *Personnel Management*, and the IPM also runs courses on the use of tests and on other selection procedures. Details of IPM courses in the use of psychological tests are available from the Institute's Course and Conference Department. Further details about leading test publishers area available in the form of an information note from the IPM's Information and Advisory Services Department. Because these details change from time to time, they are not reproduced in full in this book, but details of the suppliers of tests described in chapter 3 are given at appendix 3.

Appendix 1
Retaining or employing occupational psychologists

Personnel managers and others who anticipate large scale benefits from the introduction of testing would be well advised to seek expert advice on the choice, introduction, use, interpretation and evaluation of psychological tests.

At present, the best single guide as to whether or not an individual is expert in psychological testing for selection and assessment at work is whether he or she is a member of the Division of Occupational Psychology of the British Psychological Society; the BPS publishes a list of DOP members, and those specializing in selection methods are clearly indicated.

Dealing with members of the DOP has two further advantages. First, election to membership takes account of the width of experience of members, and this can be important if improvements in selection methods are only one of the possible ways of resolving an organization's problems. Faced with problems such as low output or high labour turnover, it is often important to identify the most cost-effective solutions and improving selection methods may or may not be the best way forward (Toplis 1970).

The second advantage is that the Division of Occupational Psychology has a code of practice designed to benefit those seeking advice from its members.

Some psychologists with considerable expertise in occupational testing and assessment are not members of the DOP and it is difficult to give simple rules as to how they can be identified. Signs include Associate Membership of the British Psychological Society to which ordinary (graduate) members of the society can be elected, active involvement in the committees of the BPS (including the Committee on Test Standards) and the publication of papers in refereed scientific journals such as the *Journal of Occupational Psychology*. A period of employment with a major employer of occupational psychologists (such as the Civil Service Commission, the Post Office, British Telecom and British Airways) might also be a good sign, as would be a period of employment in a recognized academic institution.

For organizations with large-scale programmes of staff recruitment and assessment there can be considerable advantages in employing one or more occupational psychologists, not only for the advice that they can give *vis`a vis* the organization's problems, but also the advice they can give on the many selection and assessment methods which employers are pressed to trial and use (see chapter 2). For the main part, those who design and sell unproven techniques claim little association with professional psychology in the UK and may even claim this as a merit!

Finally, remember that some people offering advice on the use of tests will be 'accredited users' (see chapter 2) whose training of several weeks will fall short of the three to five years post graduate experience required for membership of the Division of Occupational Psychology. While accredited users can have considerable experience in the use of a few tests they do not normally have the range of background information about tests or the statistical skills to give comprehensive advice.

Appendix 2
Brief overview of the theory of mental abilities

When psychological tests are mentioned the public still tends to think about intelligence or IQ tests, even though the trend for the last two or three decades has been moving away from an overall intelligence measure towards measures of more specific abilities. Even though the early intelligence tests produced one overall score, many of them had sub-scales of similar items and psychologists started looking at variations of performance across these sub-scales, even though they were not sufficiently reliable to permit worthwhile interpretation.

The evidence for the existence of a general intelligence factor came from the work of Spearman, an English psychologist, in the early 1900s. He administered a wide range of different mental ability tests to a large group of people and, after statistical analysis (correlations) of the results, found a general ability spreading across the tests. People who got higher scores on one test tended also to do well on the others, and vice-versa. The later development of a statistical technique called factor analysis, which permitted a more rigorous analysis of the results from various tests, enabled psychologists to identify much more specifically the independent factors (abilities) which are measured by a number of different tests (called a battery of tests). Unfortunately, however, different methods of factor analysis were developed and employed on different sides of the Atlantic, resulting in different results and theories of mental ability, although these differences were not completely irreconcilable.

British psychologists, notably Burt and Vernon, proposed a hierarchical structure of human abilities, with the 'g', or general intelligence factor, accounting for most variation in performance across different tests. Once the effects of 'g' have been accounted for, it is possible to find two broad (major) groups of abilities:

- v:ed — standing for verbal and educational, and covering minor group factors such as verbal, numerical, memory and reasoning abilities; and

- k:m — standing for spatial (after El Kousi, an Egyptian psychologist) and mechanical abilities, as well as perceptual (sensory) and motor skills relating to physical operations such as eye-hand co-ordination and manual dexterity.

Once the effect of these three higher level factors have been accounted for, one is left with factors which are very test specific. 'g' scores are very important for assessing someone's abilities to perform a broad range of jobs, or jobs requiring high intelligence (and also capacity to benefit from special education, eg the 11+ exam) whilst scores on minor group factors became more important for assessing people for specific jobs.

The Americans, on the other hand, as a result to some extent of their experience of using the early intelligence tests, used factor analytic methods in their research which tended to emphasise differences between mental ability factors. In 1938 Thurstone identified seven ability factors which were relatively independent, although there were modest correlations between them. He named these factors primary mental abilities:

S — Spatial ability

P — Perceptual speed

N — Numerical ability

V — Verbal meaning

M — Memory

V — Verbal fluency

I/R — Inductive reasoning

Although much research has been carried out on these primary abilities in the intervening years the results have necessitated only minor modifications to the list of primary abilities. However, results from studies using certain factor analytic methods have shown that a general factor (intelligence) does emerge which is similar to the 'g' factor. The theoretical differences across the

Atlantic are not therefore so great that they have undermined the efforts of practitioners in the assessment field.

Until the 1960s American test constructors were influenced mainly by Thurstone, their British counterparts by the work of Burt and Vernon. However, the model of human abilities devised by the American psychologist, Guilford, in the 1960s has probably had a significant influence on contemporary test constructors on both sides of the Atlantic. This model has three dimensions:

1 Mental operations:
   Cognition
   Memory
   Divergent production (thinking)
   Convergent production (thinking)
   Evaluation

2 Products:
   Units
   Classes
   Relations
   Systems
   Transfunctions
   Implications

3 Contents:
   Figural
   Symbolic
   Semantic
   Behavioural

In the model, tests have been sought to measure each cell across the three dimensions, eg a memory test dealing with classes of objects of a semantic (ie verbal nature) and so on.

At the time of his death, Guilford had claimed to have identified 98 factors out of the total possible 120 permutations across the three dimensions. His main influence on contemporary British test constructors has been on the development of tests involving different operations, relating to various ability levels of applicants; on the important differences between convergent (problem solving) and divergent (lateral, creative) thinking; and clarification of 'products' and 'contents' measured by different tests.

Appendix 3
Suppliers of tests described in chapter 3

1 EITS
Educational and Industrial Test Services Limited
83 High Street
Hemel Hempstead
Hertfordshire
HP1 3AH

2 NFER-NELSON
The NFER-NELSON Publishing Company Limited
Darville House
2 Oxford Road East
Windsor
Berks
SL4 1DF

3 SHL
Saville and Holdsworth Limited
The Old Post House
31 High Street
Esher
Surrey
KT10 9QA

4 SRA
Science Research Associates Limited
Newtown Road
Henley on Thames
Oxon
RG9 1EW

5   The Psychological Corporation
    Foots Cray High Street
    Sidcup
    Kent
    DA14 5HP

6   The Test Agency
    Cournswood House
    North Dean
    High Wycombe
    Bucks
    HP14 4NW

There are a number of other test suppliers in the UK. The Institute of Personnel Management keeps an up-to-date list of suppliers and copies can be sent to members on request.

Appendix 4
Some useful addresses

The Institute of Personnel Management
IPM House
Camp Road
Wimbledon
London
SW19 4UW

The British Psychological Society
St Andrews House
48 Princess Road East
Leicester
LE1 7DR

The International Test Commission
(J W Toplis, Secretary/Treasurer)
c/o The Post Office
Freeling House
23 Glasshill Street
London
SE1 OBQ

References

ANASTASI, A. *Psychological Testing*. 5th ed. New York, Macmillan, 1982.

AMERICAN PSYCHOLOGICAL ASSOCIATION. *Standards of Educational and Psychological Testing*. 1985.

BEDFORD, T and FELTHAM, R T. *A Cost Benefit Analysis of the Extended Interview Method*. Home Office Unit at CSSB Report No 2, 1986.

BELBIN, R M. *Management Teams: Why They Succeed or Fail*. London, Heinemann, 1981.

BENTZ, V J. 'Research findings from personality assessment of executives' in Bernadin, H G and Bownas, D A (eds). *Personality Assessment in Organizations*. New York, Praeger, 1985.

CRONBACH, L J. *Essentials of Psychological Testing*. 4th ed. New York, Harper and Row, 1984.

DULEWICZ, S V. 'Assessment centres: practical issues and research findings'. *Human Industrial Relations* (Supplement 17), 1982.

FLETCHER, C. 'Should the test score be kept a secret?' *Personnel Management*, April 1986, pp 44-46.

FLETCHER, C. 'Feedback of psychometric test results: how great is the demand?'. *Guidance and Assessment Review*. No 6, December 1985, pp 1-2.

FRENCH, C C. 'Microcomputers and psychometric assessment'. *British Journal of Guidance and Counselling*. Vol 14, No 1, 1986, pp 33-45.

GHISELLI, E E. *The Validity of Occupational Aptitude Tests.* New York, Wiley, 1966.

HUNTER, J E and SCHMIDT, F L. 'The economic benefits of personnel selection using psychological ability tests'. *Industrial Relations*, 1982.

KLINE, P. *A Handbook of Test Construction.* London, Methuen, 1986.

KLIMOSKI, R J and RAFAELI, A. 'Inferring personal qualities through handwriting analysis'. *Journal of Occupational Psychology*, Vol 56, 1983, pp 191-202.

LEWIS, C. *Employee Selection.* London, Hutchinson, 1985. (Personnel Management Series).

MILLER, K M (ed). *Psychological Testing in Personnel Assessment.* Essex, Gower Press, 1975.

McCORMICK, E J and ILGEN, D. *Industrial Psychology,* 8th ed. London, George Allen and Unwin, 1985.

MOSES, J L. 'Using clinical methods in a high level management assessment centre' in Bernadin, H G and Bownas, D S (eds). *Personality Assessment in Organizations.* New York, Praeger, 1985.

PEARN, M. *The Fair Use of Tests.* Windsor, NFER/Nelson, 1979.

ROBERTSON, I T and MAKIN, P J. 'Management selection in Britain: A survey and critique'. *Journal of Occupational Psychology,* Vol 59, No 1, 1986, pp 45-58.

RODGER, A. *The Seven Point Plan.* NFER/Nelson, Windsor, 1953.

RYNES, S L, HENEMAN, H G and SCHWAB, D P. 'Individual reactions to organizational recruiting: A review'. *Personnel Psychology,* Vol 33, 1980, pp 529-542.

SCHMIDT, F L and HUNTER, J E. 'The impact of valid selection procedures on workforce productivity'. *Journal of Applied Psychology,* Vol 64, 1979, pp 609-626.

SHACKLETON, V J and FLETCHER, C. *Individual Differences: Theories and Applications.* London, Methuen, 1984 (New Essential Psychology Series).

SMITH, M. 'Selection: where are the best prophets?' *Personnel Management,* 1986, p 63.

SOCIETY FOR INDUSTRIAL AND ORGANIZATION PSYCHOLOGY. *Principles for the Validation and Use of Personnel Selection Procedures,* 3rd ed, Maryland, University of Maryland, 1987.

STAGNER, R. 'The gullibility of personnel managers'. *Personnel Psychology.* Vol 11, 1958, pp 347-352.

STEWART, A M and STEWART, V. *Tomorrow's Managers Today.* 2nd ed. London, Institute of Personnel Management, 1981.

THORNTON, C G and BYHAM, W C. *Assessment Centres and Managerial Performance.* New York, Academic Press, 1982.

TOPLIS, J W. 'Studying people at work'. *Journal of Occupational Psychology,* Vol 44, 1970, pp 95-114.

TOPLIS, J W and STEWART, B. 'Group selection methods', in Ungerson, B (ed), *Recruitment Handbook.* 3rd ed. Hants, Gower Publishing, 1983.

TYLER, B and MILLER, K. 'The use of tests by psychologists: report on a survey of BPS members'. *Bulletin of the British Psychological Society,* Vol 39, 1986, pp 405-410.